The Politics of South China Sea Disputes

This book is a comprehensive political study of the South China Sea (SCS) disputes. With over US$5 trillion worth of trade passing through it every year and a history of military flashpoints, the SCS is invariably a hotbed of great power rivalry.

This book:

- Traces the history of the disputes from the 19th century until recent developments;
- Examines recent arbitrations, including the ruling on the case filed by the Philippines at the Permanent Court of Arbitration (PCA) at The Hague;
- Studies these disputes in a theoretical framework, utilizing international relations theories, particularly realism, liberalism and constructivism;
- Explores how the ASEAN states approach the SCS disputes and analyses dispute settlement under international law.

Drawing on extensive fieldwork and interviews with experts and those directly involved with the disputes, this book is indispensable for students and researchers of maritime studies, security studies, politics and international relations, geopolitics and Asian studies.

Nehginpao Kipgen is Associate Professor, Assistant Dean (International Collaboration) and Executive Director of Center for Southeast Asian Studies, Jindal School of International Affairs, O.P. Jindal Global University. He is the author of various books and peer-reviewed academic articles published in journals such as *Social Research, International Studies, International Journal on World Peace, World Affairs, Journal of Asian and African Studies, Journal of Muslim Minority Affairs, Ethnopolitics, India Review, Strategic Analysis, South Asia Research, Indian Journal of Political Science, Economic and Political Weekly, Asian Profile*, and *Asian Affairs*. He has published over 190 articles in leading international newspapers and magazines in five continents: Asia, Africa, Australia, Europe, and North America.

The Politics of South China Sea Disputes

Nehginpao Kipgen

Routledge
Taylor & Francis Group
LONDON AND NEW YORK

First published 2020 by Routledge

2 Park Square, Milton Park, Abingdon, Oxon OX14 4RN
605 Third Avenue, New York, NY 10017

Routledge is an imprint of the Taylor & Francis Group, an informa business

First issued in paperback 2021

Publisher's Note

The publisher has gone to great lengths to ensure the quality of this reprint but points out that some imperfections in the original copies may be apparent.

British Library Cataloguing-in-Publication Data
A catalogue record for this book is available from the British Library

Library of Congress Cataloging-in-Publication Data
A catalog record for this book has been requested

ISBN: 978-1-138-32271-4 (hbk)
ISBN: 978-1-03-217394-8 (pbk)
DOI: 10.4324/9781003026334

Typeset in Sabon
by Apex CoVantage, LLC

Contents

List of figures vi
Acknowledgments vii
Foreword ix
DANIEL C. O'NEILL
List of abbreviations xi

Introduction 1

1 A general overview of the disputes 17

2 China's claim and activities 34

3 Other claimant states and ASEAN's challenges 54

4 The July 2016 arbitral tribunal award 72

5 The role of the United States and others 89

Conclusions 105

Bibliography 114
Index 131

Figures

1.1 Overlapping claims and maritime flashpoint in the South China Sea 29
6.1 Author with Antonio T. Carpio (senior associate justice of the Supreme Court, Supreme Court of the Philippines) at his office on December 8, 2017 110
6.2 Author with Professor Robert Beckman (head, Ocean Law and Policy Programme, Centre for International Law, National University of Singapore) at his office on December 15, 2017 111
6.3 Author with Arif Havas Oegroseno (deputy coordinating minister for maritime sovereignty, Coordinating Ministry for Maritime Affairs, Government of the Republic of Indonesia) at his office in Jakarta on January 18, 2018 112
6.4 Author with Aileen Baviera (professor, Department of Political Science, University of the Philippines) at her office on December 4, 2017 112
6.5 Author with Le Hong Hiep (fellow, ISEAS-Yusof Ishak Institute, National University of Singapore) on December 22, 2017 113

Acknowledgments

This work would not have been possible without the help of many people and institutes, and I would like to take this opportunity to thank them in this journey of success. First and foremost, special thanks to O.P. Jindal Global University's Research Grant Committee for providing me the necessary financial assistance to travel to the Philippines, Singapore and Indonesia to meet several experts on the subject, including academics and government officials. I am grateful to the university library staff for supplying me books and other resources during the course of my research work.

I am very grateful to the people who agreed for interview or group discussion during my field trip: Damos Dumoli Agusman, A. Ibrahim Almuttaqi, Julio Amador, Melda Kamil Ariadno, Muhamad Arif, Rommel Banlaoi, Sidney Christopher T. Bata, Jay Batongbacal, Aileen Baviera, Robert Beckman, Antonio T. Carpio, Termsak Chalermpalanupap, Rajeev Ranjan Chaturvedy, Daniel Chua, Tan Seng Chye, Hasjim Djalal, Alberto Encomienda, Kwa Chong Guan, Wang Gungwu, Le Hong Hiep, Juwana Hikmahanto, Zhang Hongzhou, Rhodora Joaquin, Fides Quintos, Jeremy Dexter B. Mirasol, Gilang Kembara, Herman Joseph Kraft, Khanisa Krisman, Sri Nuryanti, Awani Irewati MA, Collin Koh Swee Lean, Shafiah Fifi Muhibat, Gonaranao B. Musor, Li Nan, Jaime B. Naval, Haryo Budi Nugroho, Arif Havas Oegroseno, Alcuin Papa, Rene L. Pattiradjawane, Christine Sim, Tjoki Aprianda Siregar, Jose Antonio Morato Tavares, Rafael De Bustamante Tello, Teresa Tran, Katherine Hui-Yi Tseng, Philips J. Vermonte, Dinna Wisnu and Gong Xue.

I express sincere thanks to my research assistants at the Center for Southeast Asian Studies, Jindal School of International Affairs – Soumya Chaturvedi, Devanshi Kothari and Shagun Nayar – for their research assistance and contribution. I am also thankful to Daniel O'Neill, associate professor, School of International Studies, University of the Pacific, for writing the foreword.

I remain eternally grateful to my father (L) Mangkholen Kipgen and mother Nemkhonei Kipgen for their love, support, prayers and encouragement since my earlier days of academic pursuit. They have been the backbone and inspiration to my education.

Thanks to my beloved wife Hathoihlam Kipgen and my children – Lenchung Kevin Kipgen and Thangmuan Bryan Kipgen, as well as my siblings – Nehkhokam Kipgen and his better half Veikhochin Kipgen, (L) Lhinghoineng Kipgen, Douminlal Kipgen and his better half Nengneilhing Kipgen, and Ginkhohao Kipgen – for their unfailing love and encouragement. I would also like to acknowledge the support, prayers and encouragement from friends and relatives from far and near, especially my in-laws Paukhanthang Samte and Chingngaihkim Samte, and brother in-law Mangmuanlal Samte.

Last but not least, I thank the Almighty God for giving me good health, knowledge, and the strength and perseverance that were necessary to overcome many difficulties and challenges to complete the research work and be able to publish it in a book form.

Nehginpao Kipgen

Foreword

With the possible exception of the Belt and Road Initiative, the South China Sea has been the Chinese foreign policy issue that has been subject to the greatest public interest, the most press coverage, and the largest number of books in recent years. In the summer of 2017, having just completed revisions to my own book on the subject, I crossed paths with Dr. Nehginpao Kipgen at the International Studies Association (ISA) Conference at Hong Kong University. At a panel discussion, he mentioned that he was going to write a book on the politics of the South China Sea focusing on the relations between China and ASEAN member states. I responded with a slightly sardonic comment: "Well, I've just finished writing that book, so I hope you will be taking a different approach to covering the topic."

Indeed, Dr. Kipgen has not only taken a different approach than my own political economy focus on China's use of aid, loans and investment to influence ASEAN member states, but he has also viewed the issue from a different angle than the countless recent books discussing the historical and legal aspects of the South China Sea disputes. Although he incorporates much of the extant literature in his analysis, Dr. Kipgen eschews the micro-level focus on political and economic actors taken by myself and others, as well as the legalistic approach of much of the literature from the past decade, focusing instead on what the three dominant theories in the study of international relations (IR) – realism, liberalism, and constructivism – tell us about the South China Sea disputes and what the disputes suggest about the dominant Western IR theories.

I think Dr. Kipgen might agree with me that, while it is important to know the historical and legal details of the disagreements and to understand how both international and domestic law might be applied to them, in the end, international relations are less about international laws and more about power and converting that power into influence. There is no greater evidence of this than Chinese President Xi Jinping's ability to use the promise of economic cooperation to sway Philippine President Rodrigo Duterte to ignore the ruling by the Permanent Court of Arbitration in 2016 broadly in favor of Philippine claims.

But international relations, as both liberal and constructivist scholars would argue, is not solely about power. It is also about both the perception of states by other states and the degree to which the norms and values underpinning behavior are shared. Importantly, then, in addition to utilizing the dominant Western IR theories, Dr. Kipgen incorporates the ASEAN Way, which is not only an appellation for the underlying norms of ASEAN but also an alternative, region-based view of how international relations can be constructed. In the book, he analyzes what role ASEAN has played in attempting to resolve competing claims as well as, more normatively, discussing what role ASEAN and its member states *should* play.

In addition, despite a focus on IR theories that reify the state as the primary actor in international politics, Dr. Kipgen realizes that individual leaders matter. It is hard to imagine, for example, regional politics being the same in a counterfactual world in which Xi, Duterte, and Trump were all replaced or had never taken power. Therefore, his analysis does not ignore the importance of the goals and personalities of individual leaders. I take the underlying metaphor of constructivism too far, but it is clear that as China has constructed military bases on disputed islands and constructed islands out of disputed atolls and reefs, Xi and Duterte have, nevertheless, constructed improved Sino-Philippine relations. This cooperation can be partially explained by bits and pieces of realism, liberalism and, obviously, constructivism, but it can also be partially explained by the individual motivations of the leaders of China and the Philippines, only some of which are wholly based on rational calculus to the degree that social scientists often assume.

Reason enough to read this book is that Dr. Kipgen incorporates interviews with some of the most notable experts on the South China Sea controversy from the Philippines, Indonesia, and Singapore. These insights provide much of the data he uses to test the extent to which the three IR theories and the ASEAN Way explain state and interstate behavior in the South China Sea. They will also enlighten even the most knowledgeable reader on the subject.

As it should, this book's conclusion focuses on the potential role of the oft-discussed and debated Code of Conduct (COC) as a means to manage and prevent escalation of the disputes, although not a means of actually resolving them. But, as I concluded in my own book, by ignoring the Declaration on the Conduct of Parties in the South China Sea (DOC) and asserting its sovereignty over much of the South China Sea for well over a decade, China has positioned itself to support a COC that would prevent other parties from doing what China, itself, has already accomplished: changing the status quo in the South China Sea.

Daniel C. O'Neill
September 30, 2019
Associate Professor of Political Science
School of International Studies
University of the Pacific

Abbreviations

ADMM	ASEAN Defense Ministers Meeting
ADMM Plus	ASEAN Defense Ministers Meeting plus Australia, China, India, Japan, New Zealand, ROK, the Russian Federation and the United States
AEP	Act East Policy
AMM	ASEAN Foreign Ministers' Meeting
APEC	Asia-Pacific Economic Cooperation
ARF	ASEAN Regional Forum
ASEAN	Association of Southeast Asian Nations
ASEAN+3	Association of Southeast Asian Nations plus China, Japan and South Korea
ASEM	Asia-Europe Meeting
BIMSTEC	Bay of Bengal Initiative for Multi-Sectoral Technical and Economic Cooperation
BISTEC	Bangladesh-India-Sri Lanka-Thailand Economic Cooperation
BRI	Belt and Road Initiative
CCP	Chinese Communist Party
CLCS	Convention on the Limits of the Continental Shelf
CLMV	Cambodia, Laos, Myanmar and Vietnam
CNOOC	China National Offshore Oil Corporation
COC	Code of Conduct
DOC	Declaration on the Conduct of Parties in the South China Sea
DPP	Democratic Progressive Party
EAMF	Expanded ASEAN Maritime Forum
EAS	East Asia Summit
EEZ	Exclusive Economic Zone
EU	European Union
FONOPs	Freedom of Navigation Operations
G7	Group of Seven Nations
ICJ	International Court of Justice
ITLOS	International Tribunal for the Law of the Sea
JWG	Joint Working Group
KMT	Kuomintang

LEP	Look East Policy
LOSC	Law of the Sea Convention
MJD	Minjindang
OBOR	One Belt, One Road
PCA	Permanent Court of Arbitration
PLA	People's Liberation Army
PLA-N	People's Liberation Army Navy
PNOC	Philippine National Oil Company
PRC	People's Republic of China
QSD	Quadrilateral Security Dialogue [the Quad]
ROC	Republic of China
ROK	Republic of Korea [South Korea]
SC	Security Council
SCS	South China Sea
TAC	Treaty of Amity and Cooperation
UK	United Kingdom
UN	United Nations
UNO	United Nations Organization
UNCLOS	United Nations Convention on the Law of the Sea
UNDOALS	United Nations Division for Ocean Affairs and the Law of the Sea
US	United States
US-PHL	United States–Philippines

Introduction

The South China Sea (SCS) is a semi-enclosed area, bordered in the north by China and Taiwan, the Philippines in the east, Brunei and Malaysia in the south, and Vietnam in the west. The sea is part of the Pacific Ocean, encompassing an area of about 1.4 million square miles from the Karimata and Malacca Straits to the Taiwan Strait. The SCS dispute is commonly described as one of the three flashpoints – the other two being the Korean Peninsula and the Taiwan Strait – in East Asia for a potential conflict of national interests and a threat to international peace and security. Therefore, the security issues around it always remains a focus of international attention. As a semi-enclosed area, the SCS hosts numerous islands, rocks and reefs. The major island and reef formations in the SCS are the Spratly Islands, Paracel Islands, Pratas, the Natuna Islands and the Scarborough Shoal. The sea is believed to have rich reserves of oil, natural gas and fishery stocks. It provides sea routes for maritime shipping and naval mobility. One-third of the world's shipping passes through it, carrying over US$5 trillion in trade each year. The fishery resources are particularly crucial for the food security of millions in Southeast Asia. The strategic location and the abundant resources make the sea an important agenda for diplomatic overtures among the littoral states, as well as a subject of interest and concern for the international community.

Significance and objectives of the study

The SCS disputes involve both island and maritime claims among sovereign states, and the issue has long been a point of debate in international politics. It involves not only the countries in dispute but also other major powers, including the United States (US). The important strategic location and the largely untapped abundant resources make the SCS a target of contention among the claimant states. The arbitral ruling in July 2016 gave a new momentum to the dispute. The underlying problem is the claim of overlapping areas by different countries, involving China, Brunei, Malaysia, Vietnam, the Philippines, and Taiwan. They all claim that they own the sovereignty of the islands or islets, reefs and/or resources, and so it is difficult to imagine how this protracted conflict will be amicably resolved. The disputes between China and Vietnam, and China and the Philippines, have been particularly tense in recent years.

There are several works on the SCS disputes, but they largely focus on the historical or legal perspective. This book primarily focuses on the political aspect of the disputes. The book is also different from several other works in that it is a comprehensive study covering the historical problem to the recent developments, including the 2016 arbitral ruling on a case filed by the Philippines at the Permanent Court of Arbitration (PCA) at The Hague. In this book, an attempt is made to analyze and understand some of the most critical issues of the disputes by talking to experts and people who are directly involved and/or affected by the disputes. Theoretically, an attempt is made to understand how governments and international organizations or institutions see international dispute through the lens of international relations theories, particularly realism, liberalism and constructivism. Apart from the dominant international relations theories, the book also examines the ASEAN Way as a process to understand how the Association of Southeast Asian Nations (ASEAN) states approach the SCS disputes. Though it is not the focus of this book, dispute settlement mechanism under international law is also examined.

Throughout the book, an attempt is made to address several important questions of the SCS disputes, based on interviews conducted in three countries. There are different perspectives from the core problem of the SCS to a potential solution of the disputes. The questions this book attempts to address are: What is the fundamental issue(s) of the SCS disputes? Why did the Philippines decide to pursue the case through arbitration when it was evident that China would not accept or cooperate with it? Given the arbitral ruling in favor of the Philippines, why did other claimants not pursue the same route? Can and should ASEAN play an effective role in resolving the SCS disputes? Are the Philippines and Vietnam much more vocal on the SCS disputes than the other claimants? If so, why? Why are other claimants relatively silent? Some say that the role of the US is necessary as a powers balancer, particularly to deter China. Should the US play a more active role? If so, how? What should be the role of other members of the international community, such as India, Australia, and Japan? Why is China not forcibly occupying the SCS, given its unparalleled military and economic power? Will ASEAN claimants eventually abandon their individual claims in exchange for aid and other economic assistance from China? What precisely is China's claim in the SCS, and will other claimants eventually agree to resolve the disputes through bilateral agreement, which Beijing has insisted on? As China is seemingly not interested in resolving the SCS disputes through international law, including the United Nations Convention on the Law of the Sea (UNCLOS), what is the best possible solution to the problem? And finally, what is the way forward?

It is hypothesized that claimant states are likely to accept an agreement when the application of international mechanisms serves their individual interests more than the common interests of all. One important reason why international organizations or institutions fail to deliver a mutually acceptable solution, despite the endorsement by many states, is the lack of or the absence of enforcement mechanism in the institutions to ensure effective implementation. In the SCS disputes, China's unparalleled economic and military powers have given it the advantage to ignore or disregard the interests of other claimant states and even to the extent of refusing to oblige the call for multilateralism or to respect international law.

Methodology and sources of data

The research employs the qualitative method, which involves analyzing both primary and secondary data. Primary data is collected by semi-structured interviews and discussions with over 40 experts and knowledgeable people on the SCS disputes, including government officials, academics, and legal experts in three countries – the Philippines, Singapore and Indonesia – from November 2017 to January 2018. I chose the Philippines because it is not only a claimant state but also is the state which filed a case at the PCA at The Hague. I chose Singapore partly because it was taking over the chairmanship of ASEAN from the Philippines at the beginning of 2018. Moreover, in Singapore there are several researchers and academics working on the SCS disputes. And I chose Indonesia partly because it is considered the big brother of ASEAN, and also because of the fact that it is where the ASEAN headquarters is situated. Although it does not consider itself an active claimant, Indonesia has had issues with China on the SCS. Moreover, Indonesia has several experts working on the issue. I wanted to visit all the claimant states, but it was not possible for two main reasons. First, I did not have enough financial resources. Second, I did not have enough people to talk to in countries such as China and Vietnam, which I initially considered visiting. In addition to primary data, the book also analyzes other documents, including statements released by the claimant states individually or collectively and other relevant parties and entities such as ASEAN and the European Union (EU). Secondary data is also analyzed from books, journal articles, reports, newspapers, and internet sources.

Theoretical debates

An attempt is made to understand how governments and international organizations or institutions see international dispute through the lens of international relations theories, particularly realism, liberalism and constructivism. For example, for the realists, the premise of security and order rests on military strength possessed by the state and the alliances formed by the state to ensure balance of power. The inevitable outcome of the absence of any central authority is the phenomenon of forming alliances or groups in order to protect themselves from predators. The liberalists assume that peace can be sustained in the global order with the constant engagement within the republican states, trade exchanges and interdependence under a defined body of law and a sound system of international law. Liberalism also believes that a federation of interdependent states will bring peace and ensure global security. Constructivists argue that international disputes are capable of being transformed by human practice because the SCS is socially constructed, that is, not given by nature. Though it is not an established international relations theory as such, the study also looks into the "ASEAN Way" of dispute management and how domestic politics, including personalities of leaders, play a role in the SCS disputes.

Realism

Realism as a theory emphasizes the role of the nation-state with a broad assumption that all nation-states are motivated by national interest and security in the anarchic world, and as a result there is the struggle for power (Mearsheimer 1994; Morgenthau 1948; Mowle 2003; Rose 1998; Walt 1998; Waltz 1979, 2000; Wendt 1992, 1995). The realists believe that a self-help system exists in the international relations where states seek opportunities to take advantage of each other at an opportune time. In such a dynamic matrix, the survival of a state is contingent on two strengths, that is, the material capabilities that the state inherits and the alliances that the state forms. The realists do not distinguish domestic politics from international politics but consider all forms of politics to be driven by human desires (Lebow 2013). Hans Morgenthau, a prominent realist, regards politics essentially as a struggle for power which is intrinsic to humans' social lives. According to realists, the premise of security and order rests on military strength possessed by the state and the alliances it forms to ensure balance of power. The inevitable outcome of the absence of any central authority is the phenomenon of forming alliances or groups in order to protect themselves from predators (Morgenthau 1948).

Another important understanding among the realists is the discarding of international law as it has no substantial effect, and thus, cannot be considered as proper law (Goldsmith and Posner 2005). The aspirations of a state to fulfill its national interest are unimpeded by the realm of international law when there is lack of a central authority with the power to enforce. International law becomes important only to the extent where the states form common interests or goals and define the mechanism or framework to achieve the same. For anything beyond, the international law becomes ineffective (Zangl et al. 2011). Along this line, the realists argue that the international dispute settlement mechanism is ineffective to resolve a dispute, as the mechanism falls short in ensuring compliance of the relevant international law. This inefficiency is witnessed not only in issues concerning high politics (i.e., matters that are vital to the very survival of the state such as national and international security concerns) but also in the areas of low politics (i.e., matters that are not absolutely vital to the survival of the state such as economy and social affairs), and it is often seen that the distribution of global power dictates the compliance with the dispute settlement mechanism (Posner and Yoo 2005).

The realists are, however, divided on the pattern of distribution of power that can facilitate compliance with international laws and norms. There are realists who believe in the power matrix of a hegemon. They believe that solely a hegemon can ensure compliance or enforcement of international law against the offensive state (Keohane 1980). But there are others who believe in the matrix of the balance of power. According to them, only if there exists a balance of power can the international law be applied equally over all sovereign states, including the powerful ones (Morgenthau 1948). Thus, for the international dispute settlement mechanism to thrive, it is important for a balance of power situation to exist. This could imply that in matters of low politics where a balanced distribution of power exists, compliance with an international dispute settlement mechanism may be expected. However, the compliance remains highly unattainable, although there usually is an expectation (Lebow 2013).

Realists can be either offensive or defensive. Offensive realism assumes that apart from the bipolarity situations or nuclear deterrence, security is scarce and that states want to achieve it by maximizing their relative advantage. Therefore, rational states pursuing security are prone to conflict with other states. Because of strong pressures from the international system, domestic differences do not matter much because states are under in a similar situation to act. To understand the behavior of a state, it is important to examine their relative capabilities and the external environment. States will formulate their foreign policy and promote their national interests based on these factors. On the other hand, defensive realism assumes that security is plentiful rather than scarce and states can learn from experience over time. Rational states pursuing security can be relaxed and respond only to those external threats which rarely happen. Even when such threat occurs, states respond by balancing against the threatening state(s), which then deters that state from engaging in the actual conflict. But the main exception can be when the security-seeking states fear each other and favor the offensive strategy. Under such circumstances, rational states engage in conflict when they see that there are clear incentives of doing so, that is, when the security dilemma is heightened. But such security incentives are misread or ignored by rogue states (Rose 1998).

Offensive realists see much less room for cooperation in international relations. The threatening or aggressor states may be defeated or deterred, but that does not necessarily lead to reduction of conflict. The increasing costs of war may reduce violent conflict, but rarely cooperation can be increased by changing the beliefs or information of the other states or the larger world. But for defensive realists, things depend much on the situation. Therefore, it is important and critical to study the situation and intentions of other states (Jervis 1999). The neorealists do not assume that states seek security but rather assume that states respond to the uncertainties of international anarchy by trying to control and shape their external environment. Regardless of how states try to define their national interests, the bottom line is that they are likely to increase their external influence and do everything possible to achieve it (Rose 1998).

Liberalism

Liberalism as a theory focuses, among other things, on individual freedom, political participation, equality of opportunity, human reason, and progress for peace and security (Doyle 1997; Keohane 2012). In international relations, liberalism rejects power politics as the only possible outcome of international relations and questions the security principles of realism. Liberalism emphasizes the mutual benefits of international cooperation through international organizations and non-governmental actors for shaping state preferences and policy choices. A peaceful world order is central to liberalism. And most liberalists assume that international peace and security will increase with democracy, free trade and membership in international organizations. The assumption is that democratic states are less likely to initiate or escalate conflicts or go to war with other democracies. And if states engage in international trade, the chance or likelihood of international conflict is reduced. Moreover, democratic states are more likely to cooperate and resolve differences through international institutions. Despite the varied differences among the liberalists themselves, they share a common interest on issues such as economic freedom, interdependence and international organizations (Walker and Rousseau 2016).

The liberalist understanding of international relations is a repository of analysis done by Kant, Locke and Grotius. According to Kant, peace can be sustained in the global order with constant engagement within the republican states, trade exchanges and interdependence under a defined body of law and a sound system of international law. He also believes that a federation of interdependent states will bring peace and ensure global security (Kant 1970). The liberalist assumption of the human mind marks the extreme contrast between realism and liberalism. For a liberalist, a human mind is rational, and despite self-interest-centered motivation it seeks cooperation, harmony and peaceful existence. Both in the domestic and international spheres, cooperation and harmony can be attained by revamping or modifying the structure. Kant believes that trade will expand with the growth in democracy, and as a natural outcome, the regime of international law and organizations will grow and strengthen the process of peace in the global order. Kant offers three constraints to making decisions with the potential of disrupting peace: democracy, international trade and international organization (Lebow 2013).

Democracies are believed to work on the principles of negotiation and peaceful resolution of disputes, thereby reducing the chances of escalating differences and limiting the probability of an armed conflict. Likewise, commercial interaction is considered to form the strongest link of communication, which further facilitates acknowledging cross-border identity and fostering mutual understanding. If trade facilitates peace, trade is also dependent on peace. Thus, it only acts in favor of prosperous self-interest to promote global peace. Consequently, interdependence leads to the creation of multiple global and regional level organizations, which further contribute to peace building as well as the peace preservation process.

A deeper understanding of liberalist understanding would reveal high reliance on the efficiency of the international law regime. However, such high reliance is contingent upon the existence of democracies (Slaughter 1995). In a democratic setup, the leaders are accustomed to the working of defined legal institutions, and therefore, complying with law comes naturally to such states (Moravcsik 1995). Thus, the liberalist understanding advocates that democratic states are more likely to follow international laws than the non-democratic states, which may be motivated to violate such laws to suit their individual interests (Slaughter 1995). This tendency of democracies to comply with international law would eventually mean their agreement with the international dispute settlement mechanism. The liberals, however, do acknowledge that judicialized settlement of international disputes depends on the proportion of states within the concerned organization of institutions, which are democratic in nature (Lebow 2013).

Meanwhile, the advocates of neoliberalism believe in the proposition of international law acting as an effective constraint on the behavior of a state. They believe that it is in the interest of the states to earn a good reputation by complying with international law (Guzman 2008). Another reason attributed to such compliance is to ensure credibility of the international legal regime (Cronin 2001). The neoliberalists believe in the international dispute settlement mechanism, as non-compliance will lead not only to a loss of reputation of the concerned state but will also harm the credibility of the international legal order (Simmons 2002). According to the neoliberalists, international dispute settlement mechanisms limit the behavior of the state and channelize them to ensure global peace, especially when the enforcement mechanism involves a judicial body (Smith 2000). Neoliberalism provides several venues to address territorial disputes. The first is economic liberalism, which assumes states' conscious effort to establish and deepen economic ties with whom they have engaged in territorial disputes will motivate them to find avenues for cooperation. Moreover, economic ties become powerful constraints when states decide to formulate policy, especially with states with which they are economically interdependent (Papayoanou 1996).

Another liberal theory that focuses on the central role of institution is institutional liberalism (or liberal institutionalism). It assumes that international institutions play an important role in limiting or mitigating conflicts. Although institutions may not eliminate international anarchy, they can influence the preferences and actions of states in a variety of ways, such as creating strong incentives for cooperation on trade or imposing strong disincentives such as sanctions (Navari 2008). Bilateral or multilateral institutions can be instituted to help resolve disputes through consultation, management and negotiation. Institutions offer the platform to alleviate mistrust or fear of betrayal and thus prevent states from engaging in disputes or actual wars (Choi and Eun 2018).

Over the years, there have been debates from both the liberals themselves as well as their critics about the three pillars of liberal peace, that is, democracy reducing military conflict; economic interdependence reducing military conflict; and international institutions reducing military conflict. Firstly, the liberals argue that democratic states are more likely than non-democratic regimes to resolve international disputes without resorting to the use of military force. The realists reject such claims and say that democracies are no different from the non-democracies, that is, states will balance each other through increased defense spending or by forming alliances against stronger and powerful states because of the existential perceived threat. For realists, even democratic states will engage in a balancing game and use force if and when necessary. Secondly, the liberals argue that economic interdependence in the form of flows of goods, services, capital, labor and technology will promote peace. The realists, however, counter that interdependence will increase the possibility of conflict by increasing the number of issues under competition. Thirdly, the liberals assume that international institutions decrease the likelihood of conflict. The realists reject such assumptions and argue that international institutions are either ineffective or generally the instruments of the powerful states. Overall, empirical evidence supports the claims of the liberals (Walker and Rousseau 2016).

Constructivism

The constructivist school of thought emerged as a reaction to the dominant strains of realism and liberalism in international relations. Constructivism claims that significant aspects of international relations are historically and socially constructed rather than inevitable consequences of human nature or other essential characteristics of world politics. Proponents of the theory reject the dominant assumption of the other two theories – realism and liberalism – that interest formation is a precursor to the process of social interaction among states. They believe that identity formation is a function of evolution that occurs either before or simultaneously with the formation of interests (Brunnée and Toope 2013). Constructivists also challenge what is assumed to be a realist view about the state and demonstrate that there is a possibility of collective identities transcending international borders where international institutions play an important role (Palan 2000).

Although constructivists acknowledge that interest and power are important, they tend to focus on variables such as social norms, ideas, culture, history and narratives and their impact on identity and behavior formation. Thus while analyzing the role of and interaction among actors and institutions, constructivism as a school of thought provides useful and compelling insights. Constructivists brought to light a sharp critique of material security and interest which was a dominant assumption of the realists and liberals. According to constructivists, the core of international relations is the factor of social dimension and the dynamic nature of relationships among states. They believe in the idea of dialogue between states that is specific to historical and cultural circumstances, and therefore, these become crucial in understanding relations. Constructivists also believe that international relations is a social construct. For instance, social phenomena such as the state, alliances and so forth may be born out of human nature in the study of international relations, but they are constructed to take particular forms due to historical, social, cultural or political reasons due to the interaction of states with each other. The constructivists disregard the notion of a single objective reality. They intend to draw different factors together and explain or understand the change of events. While concentrating on the social dimensions of international relations, they highlight the importance not only of laws but also norms, rules and customs. They also focus on interaction. This process of interaction, according to them, is embedded in historical, political, cultural and other such realities. The constructivists argue that the social interaction produces a space of choice for the participants which further develops their relationship. Since these participants share a social relationship, their choices are partially dependent on the expected response of the other (Fierke 2013).

The preceding analysis entails that for a constructivist, the concept of national identity would mean more than values prescribed by the nation. It will form the national interest of the state and dictate the way in which the state will behave in the wider world (Hopf 1998). Therefore, the identity and interest of a nation which is defined by its social, cultural, historical and political experiences become important considerations while discussing the settlement of international disputes. These ideational values also play an important source in identifying the source of a dispute and the mechanism to deal with such disputes (Wendt 1992). The notion of power and interest as suggested by realism and liberalism are inefficient in answering why disputes linger or remain unresolved. This is answered by constructivism while considering social facts such as historical or cultural attachment or other such instinctive tendencies (Buss 1995; Choi and Eun 2018). It can also be embedded in the collective conscience of the society or cultural or traditional societal knowledge. Another important ideational value that plays a significant role in world politics and dispute settlement is that of norms.

These norms can be defined as practices or behaviors that are collectively described as legitimate by individuals belonging to a particular identity (Choi and Eun 2018). Norms play a fundamental role in prescribing acceptable standards of behavior for states, and at the same time they provide constraints on the behavior.

According to Jong Kun Choi and Yong-Soo Eun, three concrete measures can be taken to address an international dispute under the constructivist school of thought. They are the development of benign norms, cooperative norms and intersubjective identities, and discourses (Choi and Eun 2018). Benign norms can significantly alter the perception toward the issue, the plausible solutions and the final decision. Such norms will disincentivize adverse behavior as states share mutually constitutive behavior in a social matrix. The second alternative is to develop intersubjective identities where there is space to provide a common understanding of the activities and intentions of the parties to a dispute. This helps in identifying alliances and adversaries of the states. In such scenarios, the sharing of intersubjective identities leads to harmonious resolution of disputes. The third and the most important constructivist measure to address an international dispute is through organized discourses. Choi and Eun believe that discourses provide the platform needed to share benign norms and formulate intersubjective identities. Discourses assist in remolding the identities and interests of states. Discourses also have the inherent capacity to define interests in a manner where they can potentially affect behavior. This would entail that if discourses can create a community of shared identity and interest, they will influence and reshape the behavior of states within the community. This will further act as a deterrence to states from resorting to aggressive or violent actions. These discourses can be organized in both top-down and bottom-up approaches. While top leaders and policy makers are involved in the former, the latter witnesses the participation of civil society organizations and other grassroot-level players. This also facilitates creating a confidence-building framework which encourages conflict prevention and dispute settlement (Choi and Eun 2018).

The ASEAN Way

The ASEAN Way is basically a method or an approach to address issues in Southeast Asia by ASEAN members. It primarily has two components. The first part is the emphasis on decision-making through informal consultations by diplomats with the goal of reaching a consensus agreement at the official meetings. The second part is governed by a set of issues in the Treaty of Amity and Cooperation (TAC), which includes respect for state sovereignty, freedom from external interference, non-interference in internal affairs, peaceful dispute settlement, renunciation of the use of force, and cooperation. Although the principles of consultation, consensus and non-interference entail that ASEAN focuses only on issues all members can agree upon, it is also true that the adherence to such principles is essential for the region's stability. It is also evident that the different regime types within ASEAN make it difficult to establish any coordinated efforts, not to mention formulating a common agenda (Leviter 2010). However, there may be situations where a consensus does not necessarily require unanimity, and decisions may be taken with misgivings from one or more states as long as such decisions do not damage the interests of dissenting members (Seah 2009).

The ASEAN Way is more about management and containment of problems. The process of consultation is an indication of a desire to first establish an intramural environment to address the actual conflicts. In other words, conflicts are dealt internally through quiet diplomacy by setting aside the difficult issues so that they do not stop or hinder the progress on other areas of cooperation. There are three key principles all ASEAN member states follow to ensure the organization's success. The first is restraint, which refers to a commitment to the policy of non-interference in the internal affairs of member states. The second is respect, which needs to be pursued by frequent consultation among member states. The third is responsibility, which means that each member state should consider the interests and concerns of other fellow member states. The adoption of a consensus agreement, which is slow and at times difficult, is usually the lowest common denominator among member states. But the sustenance of a consensus policy is also essential for maintaining coherence among ASEAN states which are politically, economically and religiously diverse. The ASEAN Way shows that the organization is effective and productive when the national interests of member states coincide. When such situation is not possible, they at least attempt to create the appearance of unity despite their internal differences (Narine 1997).

When the TAC was signed by the founding members of ASEAN in 1976, the objective was to promote perpetual peace, everlasting amity and cooperation among the people of Southeast Asia, which would contribute to their strength, solidarity and closer ties. The adoption of TAC was significant particularly for the fact that it is legally binding on all its signatories against both forcible and non-forcible intervention. The ratification of TAC is an indication of ASEAN members' endorsement and commitment to the rule against non-intervention in the affairs of member states. The TAC provides some form of legal protection to all its signatories as well as a common or collective identity to the Southeast Asian states, which is important especially for the smaller states in the midst of anarchy in international politics. Over the years, the interpretation of forcible or non-forcible intervention has become less stringent, particularly on the issue of human rights. Nevertheless, the ASEAN member states continue to believe that the policy of non-intervention remains fundamentally important to their national interests. As ASEAN gradually matures, its preference of loose arrangements over legally binding documents has created practical problems for its efforts toward regional integration, especially regarding the economy (Seah 2009).

Despite its shortcomings and challenges, ASEAN has remained largely peaceful not only among themselves but also with others in the region and around the world by adhering to the principles of peaceful settlement of disputes, rejection of the threat or use of force, and the non-intervention in the internal affairs of member states. ASEAN has also been successful in persuading other non-regional countries to accede to its TAC. When it comes to bilateral territorial disputes, the ASEAN states have in the past approached the International Court of Justice (ICJ) and the International Tribunal for the Law of the Sea (ITLOS) and have complied with their rulings. The High Council, as provided in the TAC, for the formation of a ministerial-level body to help find a peaceful settlement of disputes has not been used. And for regional security and peace, all ASEAN members are bound by the TAC not to develop, manufacture or acquire, possess or have control of nuclear weapons; transport any nuclear weapons; or test or use nuclear weapons in the Southeast Asian region. One good example of the success of the ASEAN Way is that 10 of the 11 countries in Southeast Asia are now members of the regional bloc which was initially started in 1967 by five members: Indonesia, Malaysia, the Philippines, Singapore and Thailand. The diplomatic success of ASEAN, among others, is the creation of the ASEAN Regional Forum (ARF), which deals with peace and security issues of the larger Asia Pacific region, with the participation of 27 countries around the world (Severino 2007).

Conflict studies provide some foundation for understanding the ASEAN Way of conflict management. The ASEAN approach to conflict management has been based on certain principles, including consensus, consultation, informal and bilateral meeting, and non-interference in the affairs of member states. There are two fundamental areas where management of disputes has been identified. The principles, norms and codes of conduct are first identified in interstate behavior and then in the decision-making processes. The primary guiding principle of interstate behavior is non-intervention, and the decision-making processes follow the principles of consultation and consensus agreement. Member states comply with the principles of non-intervention, consultation and consensus agreement even when they are not formally promulgated or codified. Consultation and consensus decision-making processes give the opportunity for ASEAN to avoid or reconcile their differences, which can potentially cause conflict among member states. However, there are criticisms that the ASEAN Way of security arrangement is weak and vulnerable in cases of extra-regional or intrastate conflicts, in which the wider international community may see the need for external intervention, such as the case of the East Timor dispute, which Indonesia considered as its internal issue of sovereignty and territorial integrity but attracted wider international concerns (Nishikawa 2007).

International law

Churchill and Lowe in *The Law of the Sea* discuss settlement of disputes under a few important concepts – consensual settlement, compulsory settlement obligations, compulsory dispute settlement and provisional measures. Article 279 and 280 of the 1982 Law of the Sea Convention (LOSC) stipulate that states have the right to settle any dispute between them by peaceful means, including dispute settlement between states and non-state entities on issues such as the international sea bed authority and the enterprise, and the deep-seabed mining companies. In case the parties in dispute cannot reach a peaceful settlement under the agreed procedures, one of the parties may invite the other to submit to the conciliation procedure as stated in Article 284 of the LOSC. If such invitation is accepted, each party chooses two conciliators each, and then the four select the fifth conciliator who acts as chairman of the conciliation panel. But when the two parties are unable to find a peaceful settlement under their own freely chosen panel, the provision of compulsory dispute settlement is considered. If a party to the dispute declares that it will not accept compulsory dispute settlement over the boundaries of its territorial seas, Exclusive Economic Zone (EEZ) or continental shelf, either of the parties may insist that the matter be referred to compulsory conciliation. The two parties are obliged to continue negotiation on the basis of the report furnished by the conciliation commission. Otherwise, they should agree to some other procedures for dispute settlement. The disputing parties are given considerable freedom in choosing the compulsory procedures, such as the ITLOS, the ICJ, an Annex VII arbitral tribunal and an Annex VIII special arbitral tribunal (Churchill and Lowe 1999).

The ITLOS was established under Annex VI of the LOSC and has 21 members with competence on law of the sea, who are elected by members of the convention to have a representative body of all the world's important legal systems. The tribunal's quorum in a plenary session is 11, which means all members do not necessarily have to be present in the deliberation process. The tribunal is empowered to function with special chambers of three or four members and may also work through the 11-member seabed disputes chamber. The next procedure, the ICJ, whose judges consist of lawyers of the highest reputation, is a powerful body in the sense that the court's jurisdiction cannot be withdrawn once the proceeding has begun against the state. Any refusal would prevent arbitration of the issue, since arbitration depends on the willingness of both parties to agree to participate in the arbitral process. Even cases arising out of the interpretation or application of international treaties may be referred to the court. However, the ICJ has often been criticized for its inability to bring on board states that are reluctant to appear before its panel (Churchill and Lowe 1999).

The third procedure is arbitral tribunals under Annex VII of LOSC, which deals with disputes between states or disputes involving international organizations. Arbitrators must have some level of experience in maritime affairs, but not necessarily on the law of the sea. The fourth procedure is the special arbitral tribunals under Annex VIII of the LOSC, which deals with four categories of specialized disputes: fisheries, environmental protection, maritime scientific research and navigation. These tribunals may be used as fact-finding commissions to explore and examine facts relating to the disputes under the four specialized areas. However, establishment of such a fact-finding commission should be done with the consent of both parties. The disputing parties may also choose other options such as negotiation or arbitration for dispute settlement. Another procedure to settle international disputes is through provisional measures. Under such circumstances, it is possible that "one of the disputing parties is proposing to take action which would prejudice the rights of the other even if the dispute were ultimately to be settled on the other's favour" (Churchill and Lowe 1999, 459).

Surya P. Subedi in *Resolution of International Water Disputes: Challenges for the 21st Century* explains the importance of bilateral or regional treaties in addressing, if not settling, international water disputes under the 1997 United Nations Convention on the Law of the Non-navigational Uses of International Watercourses (UN Watercourses Convention). But such course of action can be taken as the last resort "only in the absence of an applicable bilateral or regional agreement" between the disputing parties (Subedi 2003, 34). A peaceful means of dispute settlement, such as diplomatic means, negotiation by good offices, mediation and conciliation through the involvement of a third party should be explored. Although it is not mandatory to bring disputes to ICJ or an arbitration tribunal, they serve as other options for the concerned states to address disputes. Under the Watercourses Convention, if a dispute is not resolved within six months by the concerned parties, either through negotiation or other peaceful means of bilateral agreement, the dispute must be submitted to an impartial fact-finding at the request of any of the disputing parties. The Watercourses Convention allows the disputing parties to explore different channels of diplomatic and judicial remedial measures, including the PCA (Subedi 2003).

Organization of the book

There are seven chapters in this book. The introduction discusses the significance and objectives of the study, research questions and the hypothesis, and the methodology and sources of data. It analyzes the theoretical debates on how governments and international organizations or institutions see international disputes through the lens of established international relations theories, particularly realism, liberalism and constructivism. It also analyzes the ASEAN Way of dispute management, and dispute settlement under international law.

The objective of Chapter 1 is to discuss the general overview of the SCS disputes from ancient times to the present day, without specifically focusing on any single claimant state. Based on interviews in three different countries, the chapter elaborates on what is considered to be the fundamental issue(s) of the SCS disputes.

Chapter 2 specifically examines China's claim and activities in the SCS since ancient times to the present day. It discusses the claim and activities of the People's Republic of China (PRC), including its artificial island buildings and the ramifications, its bilateral engagement with other claimant states, and with ASEAN. Based on interviews, the chapter attempts to answer what precisely is China's claim in the SCS. Also based on responses from the interviewees, this chapter analyzes why China is not forcibly occupying the SCS, given its unparalleled military and economic power.

Chapter 3 attempts to understand the claims and activities of other claimant states (other than China) – Taiwan, the Philippines, Vietnam, Malaysia, and Brunei – as well as the efforts and challenges of ASEAN as a collective body. Based on interviews, the chapter addresses questions such as whether the Philippines and Vietnam are much more vocal on the SCS disputes than the other claimants. If so, why are other claimant states relatively silent? The chapter also addresses other questions, such as whether ASEAN should play an effective role in resolving the SCS disputes, whether the ASEAN claimants will eventually abandon their individual claims in exchange for aid and other economic assistance from China, and whether all claimants will eventually agree to resolve the disputes through bilateral agreement which Beijing has been insisting upon. It then analyzes the position of Indonesia vis-à-vis the SCS disputes despite being a non-active claimant state. The chapter also examines the initiatives taken by ASEAN over the years from the 2002 non-binding Declaration on the Conduct of Parties (DOC) to the 2017 Code of Conduct (COC).

Chapter 4 examines the circumstances and events leading up to the July 2016 arbitration and its effects, both positive and negative. It analyzes the positions and arguments of both the Philippines and China before and after the arbitration. The chapter incorporates the responses of several interviewees on questions such as: Why did the Philippines decide to pursue the case through arbitration when it was evident that China would not accept or cooperate with it? And given the arbitral ruling in favor of the Philippines, why did other claimants not pursue the same route?

The objective of Chapter 5 is to understand the role of the US and other countries which are not direct claimants in the SCS disputes. The role of the US, which basically demands freedom of navigation and overflight, is emphasized as some of the claimant states see it as the only country that can balance China. Some say that the role of the US is necessary as a power balancer, particularly to deter China. Should the US play a more active role? If so, how? The chapter also examines the role of other neighboring naval power, such as India, Australia, and Japan.

The conclusion chapter summarizes the major points of the book, and discusses the linkage of IR theories and ASEAN Way with the research findings and attempts to theorize. It also discusses the way forward in the SCS disputes. Since China is seemingly not interested in resolving the SCS disputes through international law such as the UNCLOS, what is the best possible solution to the problem? Based on existing literature and the research findings, the conclusion presents the author's own analysis of the problem and its future prospects.

1 A general overview of the disputes

The precolonial and colonial times

The SCS had a different purpose than to simply claim resources that were available on the islands. It used to serve as a mode of communication, calling on the ports of many great dynasties. The SCS had two sailing routes that went in opposite directions. The main route flowed from Taiwan to Luzon and down to Palawan, Borneo. Ships avoided the central area and instead sailed along the inhabited coasts. It was essential for the ships navigating these routes to avoid the continuous zone of danger, now known as the Spratly and Paracel Islands (Gungwu 1998). Earliest trading records dates back to the 8th century when Sri Vijaya, a maritime and commercial kingdom, largely based in what is now known as Indonesia, ruled the Straits of Malacca till the 12th century. It was only after this that the Chinese commercial and naval forces expanded under the expeditions of Admiral Zheng He (Levathes 1994). Trading ships from the West arrived in the region in the 16th century to capitalize on regional trade and profit from their skills. European merchant companies also took home spices and ceramics from the locals, and slowly took control over ports and cities from the Arabs who had been key in making Malay the official language for communication over long distance trade (Blussé 1996).

In the 15th and 16th centuries, the Europeans advanced their explorations in three main areas: the Atlantic basin from the Atlantic islands and coastal western Africa to the hinterlands of the American continents; the northern seas stretching from the Baltic Sea to the White Sea and the Siberian coast and to the coasts of Canada; and then to the Oriental seas and northern Asia. The Pacific region came under European control during the 18th century following the occupation of islands and coastal areas of the western Pacific such as Australia, New Zealand, New Guinea and the Pacific islands. When the Europeans arrived in Southeast Asia in the 15th century, the region was open, wealthy and vibrant. The context and situation changed as the intention of the Europeans shifted from acquiring trade concessions in the huge markets of Southeast Asia and China to extracting minerals and growing crops for export, further encroachment into Asia and the prestige of political and legal legitimacy. By the end of the 19th century, the Europeans had already established their footprint across the globe economically, militarily and culturally as well as through religious activities. By the mid-19th century, the effort to establish international cooperation and management in maritime affairs took on new momentum with the Declaration of Paris of 1856. The International Convention for the Protection of Submarine Cables was signed in 1884 by 26 states to regulate international communication and vessel operations. Subsequently in 1889, a conference on safety at sea was convened in Washington to deliberate on important but difficult issues, such as the rules to determine the worthiness of vessels and compulsory sea lanes in frequented waters, and the idea of creating a permanent international maritime committee, a predecessor of today's the International Maritime Organization (Tseng 2017).

Maritime claims often involve sovereignty dispute. Stein Tønnesson discussed three ways of understanding a sovereignty dispute. The first is a national perspective which goes back as far as possible in history to find evidence that the area in question has been part of its territory and how sovereignty has been maintained through prescription, occupation and utilization. The second is about presenting the chronology of the conflicting claims and accordingly exploring a possible solution through international law. The third option is to treat the dispute as part of international history and analyze it on the basis of the changing international system and the balance of power. Historical records play vital role in addressing a sovereignty dispute. It is important and in fact normal for states to present critical dates when there are competing states asserting or reiterating their claims. In the case of the SCS disputes, particularly the Spratlys and the Paracels, the critical years of the different claimants are 1877, 1909, 1933, 1946–1947, 1951–1952, 1956, 1971, 1974, 1982–1983 and 1988. The history of the dispute started in the 19th century with the European colonial powers dividing territories among states which enjoyed full sovereignty. Mapping and demarcation of land borders between the Southeast Asian states started in the mid-19th century, but maritime delimitation is more of a recent development. Historically, the function of the SCS was mainly about communication. Both small and large ships from many countries passed through the sea for more than 2,000 years and had called on ports controlled by several dynasties and states. Income generated from trade passing through the SCS had helped sustain many of the powerful states, such as Funan, Angkor, Sri Vijaya, Ayutthaya, Champa and the Melaka Sultanate. For the mainland Southeast Asian states, the trade route passing through the coast of China past Taiwan and Hainan, down the coast of Indochina, and then across the Gulf of Thailand to the Malacca Straits was hugely vital for economic sustenance. The rulers were able to collect taxes from ships that passed by (Tønnesson 2002).

The history of the SCS disputes actually began in the 19th century. By introducing the concept of national sovereignty to a region that had not developed the idea of legal claims, the British and the French led the colonial movement, fundamentally changing the political geography of Asia. By dividing sovereign states on the basis of territory, new colonial states were constructed. The Opium War against China (1839–1842), the acquisition of Hong Kong as a colony, the establishment of protectorates in Malaya and Borneo and the construction of a port city called Singapore were all in tandem with the British conquest. After the British took Melaka from the Dutch in 1975, it prompted the latter to strengthen and integrate the states it had occupied, and to name it the Netherlands Indies, which later became Indonesia. After witnessing Britain become a leading merchant of the era, Spain tightened its hold on the Philippines. France, in its ambition to become a global hegemon, chose to colonize Indochina (1863–1884) in order to compete with the British in their trade with China and also to protect Christianity. The end of the 19th century saw the establishment of new colonies around the SCS by two formidable powers: Japan and the US. Japan's victory in the Sino-Japanese War in 1895 ceased China's attempt to establish itself as a naval power and acquired Taiwan in the peace settlement that followed. The Spanish-American War of 1898 resulted in the ouster of the Spanish from the Philippines (Wu and Zou 2016).

The Europeans and the Americans at first saw the small islets in the central part of the SCS as a source of danger and did not show much interest in them. New maps were drawn in Europe, Japan, Korea, and America which showed that the Spratlys and the Paracels were two separate archipelagos. The eastern half of the Spratlys was marked off on the British maps as a dangerous area. While the commercial and naval ships avoided the two archipelagos, oceanographers were sent to conduct surveys and found that the islands were inhabited during some parts of the year by fishermen, most of whom spoke Hainanese dialects and lived some parts of the year in Hainan itself. Captain Spratly gave the island his own name. The British made formal claim on the Spratlys and Amboyna Cay in 1877, which was probably the first time any state made a modern legal claim to any of the Spratly or Paracel Islands. From 1891 to 1933, both the Spratlys and Amboyna Cay were mentioned annually in the British colonial office list, although little was done to exploit them or assert their sovereignty. Though the Paracels were larger and occupied a more strategic shipping route from Singapore to Hong Kong, no European state made any formal claim before the 1930s. In 1909, it was the Chinese that showed an interest in the islands by sending a mission there. But during the next three decades, the Qing dynasty succumbed to the Chinese revolution; China fell apart, and as a result, it was in no position to maintain its claim on the Paracels and other smaller islands such as the Pratas and reef in the southwest of Taiwan and the southeast of Hong Kong. Following the invasion of Manchuria in 1932, Japan became the rising power in the SCS region. Though Japan did not make any legal claim, the Japanese merchants competed with the Europeans and the Americans. Between 1930 and 1933, France formally claimed the

Spratlys and occupied some of them. After the Sino-Japanese War in 1938, France formally claimed the Paracels and established a permanent presence alongside the Japanese forces who had already established a base there. Though the British did not oppose the French actions, they did not abandon the Spratly Islands and Amboyna Cay (Tønnesson 2002).

The SCS disputes, which have existed for over 80 years, involve both maritime boundaries and islands which have gone through different twists and turns. France invaded the Paracel Islands in 1925, which resulted in a territorial dispute over the Paracels between France and China in 1931. It was then followed by a dispute over the Spratly Islands among China, Japan and France starting in 1933. In December 1934, the Review Board of the Water and Land Map of China passed a resolution confirming that the Spratly and Paracel Islands belonged to China and published a formal map of four island groups in the SCS. Japan then dispatched its troops to occupy the Spratly Islands in January 1939. The government of France demanded that the International Court of Arbitration handle the disputes, but the proposal was rejected by Japan. In March 1939, Taiwan stated that the Spratly Islands were under the administration of the Office of the Governor-General of Taiwan and were named the Shinnan Islands district, Kaohsiung city, Kaohsiung country. On March 31, 1939, the Japanese government informed the French embassy in Japan of its annexation of the Spratly Islands, but France and the UK opposed the announcement. Later in December 1947, the Chinese government proclaimed the reintegration of the Spratly and Paracel Islands into its administrative jurisdiction (Chen 2014).

On June 7, 1933, when there were rumors about the French taking control of the Spratlys, China established the Review Committee for Land and Water Maps. While the committee was deliberating its options, a cartographer named Chen Duo published a new atlas which stretched the Chinese border to 7 degrees north latitude, which included the Spratly Islands that France claimed. The publication may have influenced the Review Committee for Land and Water Maps because its response to the French claim came about after a study of a year and a half. In its first journal published in January 1935, the committee included 132 islands and islets on the SCS which it claimed rightfully belonged to China, of which 28 were in the Paracels and 96 in the Spratlys. The list did not comprise Chinese names but rather transliterations and translations from the Western names printed on the navigation charts. Three months later, in April 1935, the committee published *The Map of Chinese Islands in the South China Sea*, taking the country's sea border to 4 degrees north latitude, which was 107 kilometers from the coast of Borneo and over 1,500 kilometers from the Chinese mainland. Then an eminent Chinese geographer, Bai Meichu, came up with his own map, the *Chinese National Humiliation Map*, to educate his countrymen of how much territory they had lost. His 1936 *New China Construction Atlas* included a U-shaped line around the SCS as far as James Shoal, which was copied by others. Between 1936 and 1945, versions of the map were published in other

26 maps, with some stretching down to James Shoal, though most included only the Spratlys. A decade later, the Chinese government used Bai Meichu's map as the basis for its historical claim for island territories. List-making and map drawing came to an end with the Japanese invasion of China in 1937. Since Japan had occupied Taiwan in 1895, the entire coast of the SCS from Taiwan to Singapore fell under its control, especially after the surrender of the American forces in the Philippines in May 1942. The SCS became a "Japanese lake" and remained so until January 1945 (Hayton 2014).

Japan's advancement in the SCS during the 1930s was a result of interacting factors. The first was due to the rise of the military after the navy played an important role in the decision-making process. The navy called for increasing the military budget. Though there was a naval ratio of 10–10–7 between the US, UK and Japan during the 1930 conference on naval limitation in London in 1930, the Ministry of the Navy requested its withdrawal from the 1921 Five Power Treaty on limiting naval armament on December 31, 1936. Subsequently, the navy and army pressed for the protection of the Japanese empire in the Far East by expanding military power. Both the army and the navy proposed a national policy plan emphasizing the importance of Southeast Asia. At a joint meeting between the prime minister, the army, the navy and the foreign ministry in August 1936, the new version of the national policy plan, the basis of national policy, reiterated the need to maintain military superiority in the Southeast Asia region. The military expansion was intertwined with economic and social factors. The economic development was tied to the broadening of activities in the east, southeast and Pacific Ocean waters. The Japanese fishermen caught crab and salmon in the northern Pacific Ocean, the Alaskan region in the northeast, and in Micronesia in the central Pacific region. Overall, the Japanese policy was to preserve peace in the east to exploit the resources and to guarantee economic and political privileges in the region. However, it was during the political instability period in Japan, beginning in 1933, that the conflict over the Spratlys and the Paracels began (Granados 2008).

Table 1.1 Colonial occupation of the South China Sea Islands – Meiji, Taisho periods

Year	*Parties*	*Archipelago*	*Activity*	*Notes*
Meiji 35 (1902)	Tamaoki Han'emon	Pratas Islands	Survey	Claimed discovery in 1901
Meiji 35	Nishizawa Yoshiji	Pratas Islands	Survey	
Meiji 38 (1905)	The Tsunenobu Trading Co.	Pratas Islands	Survey	Requested incorporation into the empire

(*Continued*)

Table 1.1 (Continued)

Year	*Parties*	*Archipelago*	*Activity*	*Notes*
Meiji 40 (1907)	Koshinsha Co.	Pratas Islands	Survey	
Meiji 40	Mizutani Shinroku, Nishimura Takezo	Pratas Islands	Survey	Requested incorporation into Taiwan authority
Meiji 40	Nishizawa Yoshiji	Pratas Islands	Survey (second)	Renamed islands
Since Taisho 6 (1917)	Ishimaru Shosuke, Matsushita Giichiro	Pratas Islands	Fishery	
Showa 6 (1931)	Wasa Kichisaburo, Higashihama Mitsuaki	Pratas Islands	Fishery	Arrested by Chinese authorities
Taisho 6 (1917)	Komatsu Shigetoshi Ikeda Kinzo	Paracel Islands Spratly Islands	Survey	
Taisho 6-8 (1917-1919)	Hirata Sueji	Paracel Islands Spratly Islands	Survey (3 times)	Claimed discovery of the Paracels. Named as Hirata Archipelago
Taisho 7 (1918)	Kamoshita Matsujiro, Sakurai Ryosuke	Spratly Islands	Survey	Government employees
Taisho 8 (1919)	Kamiyama Keiji, Hashimoto Keizaburo	Paracel Islands (?) Spratly Islands (?)	Survey	Economic development petitioned
Since Republic of China year 10 (1921)	He Ruinian (China-Macau?) Liang Guozhi (China?)	Paracel Islands	Phosphate recollection	Japanese investment
Taisho 12 (1923)	Hirata Sueji	Paracel Islands	Phosphate recollection	
Taisho 9 (1920)	Aito Eikichi, Nozawa Senzo, Yamazaki Takeshi	Spratly Islands (12 islands)	"Discovery," survey the following year	Economic development petitioned
Taisho 7 (1918)	Lhasa Phosphates Co.	Spratly Islands	Secret survey	
Taisho 9-10 (1920-1921)	Lhasa Phosphates Co.	Spratly Islands	Survey (second)	Renamed islands as New South Archipelago
Since Taisho (1923)	Lhasa Phosphates Co.	Spratly Islands	Survey (third), phosphate recollection	

Source: Granados (2008, 127–128).

Decolonization and Cold War Era, 1942–1968

During World War II, Japan occupied the Paracel and Spratly Islands and annexed them with the administrative jurisdiction of Taiwan. At the end of World War II, the San Francisco Peace Treaty was signed in 1951 and the Sino-Japanese Peace Treaty the following year. Both treaties stipulated that Japan renounce its right, title and claim to the Paracel and the Spratly Islands. The purpose of the San Francisco Peace Treaty, mostly between Japan and the Allied powers, was to deprive Japan of its occupied territories before and during the war and to find a way to peacefully coexist. Since there were different views about the Paracel and the Spratly Islands, a resolution was made that Japan renounce the islands to avoid controversy, without giving sovereign authority to any single country, which would make it possible for any powerful country to claim at any given moment (Chen 2014). The main effect of World War II was the destruction of the colonial era and the introduction of a new international system of independent states. At least on paper, Japan was able to fulfill its promise of granting independence to the Philippines, Indonesia, Vietnam, Cambodia and Laos (Tønnesson 2002).

The period from 1942 to 1968 saw a different framework of international relations around the SCS. The colonial order was supplanted by an arrangement of new autonomous states, separated against each other by contrary belief systems and frosty wartime partnerships. The period began with the British inability to guard Singapore against Japanese attack and ended with the British choosing to pull back from east of Suez. Toward the end of the period, the US emerged as the main maritime power. In 1941, Japan had entered into a treaty of co-operation with the French administration in Indochina, which enabled Japan to utilize Indochina's ports and landing strips for the 1942 attack on the British and Dutch settlements. During a great part of World War II, the French and Japanese troops lived next to each other in the Paracels. But after the Japanese defeated the French in Indochina in 1945, the French-Vietnamese troops pulled back. By that time, the US had established itself as the predominant maritime power in the Asia Pacific (Tønnesson 1991).

While the US was involved in the Vietnam War, Britain directed establishment of an anti-communist Malaysian federation, comprising Malaya, Sabah and Sarawak as well as Singapore. The formation of Malaysia in 1963 incited a low-scale military showdown with Indonesia, which ended when the anti-communist faction of the Indonesian armed forces seized control of Jakarta in 1965. This gave the political premise to the establishment of a non-communist ASEAN in 1967, comprising Indonesia, Malaysia, the Philippines, Singapore and Thailand. In this way, another worldwide framework had been established in the area comprising, on one hand, five non-communist states with different connections toward the Western forces, and on the other hand, a troubled Indochina. The fruitful British decolonization, and a solid US responsibility regarding shielding the non-communist states, made it workable for Britain to take the monetarily vital choice in mid-1968 to end its military presence in Asia (Pickering 1998).

After 1948–1949, the procedure of decolonization coincided with Cold War considerations. What brought the Cold War to Asia was the triumph of the communists in the Chinese Civil War and the founding of the PRC in 1949 under Chairman Mao Zedong. In 1950, Mao signed a treaty of alliance with the Soviet Union, the primary enemy of the US-driven Western alliance on a worldwide scale. Mao's triumph and the Sino-Soviet treaty started fears that socialism would spread to other Asian nations. The communist challenge was not a maritime one, rather it was a risk of famous uprisings due to supply of arms and hardware from China and the Soviet Union. The fundamental maritime aspect of the Cold War in Southeast Asia was an emerging dispute over the movement of arms. Weapons, drugs and other supplies were brought to the rebellion movements from China and other places. The British, French and American naval forces checked interchanges adrift and monitored communications (Murfett et al. 1999). From the Japanese surrender in 1945 to the end of the Vietnam War in 1975, the US was largely the most grounded maritime power in the Pacific region. China did not have the ability to extend maritime power past its beachfront waters, and regardless of the Sino-Soviet treaty, the Soviet naval force did not set up any critical bases on Chinese soil. The US was invariably in control of the ocean and the air. The procedures of decolonization and the Cold War were accompanied by the emergence of a new region called Southeast Asia (Tønnesson 1991).

The fundamental concern of the US, as the main maritime power, was to prevent the spread of socialism. The US was not necessarily interested in occupying or dominating the islets – the Spratlys and the Paracels – except as occasional targets for artillery exercises. As before the war, the US declined to help competing claims in the islands. At the same time, there was no country which could provoke or challenge the US maritime power in the SCS. The primary US concern was the freedom of passage through the sea. Freedom of navigation was even more imperative for Japan, once a wartime adversary but later a dedicated partner of the US. Japan adopted the 1920s strategy of business development and benefited significantly from the repercussions of the Korean and Vietnam Wars. Japan became a major destination of oil shipments from the Middle Eastern countries through the SCS. The most dynamic claimant to the islands following World War II was the Republic of China (ROC) – under the administration of Chiang Kai-shek – which sent maritime endeavors to both the Paracels and the Spratlys in 1946–1947 and set up territorial markers, and built up a permanent establishment on Itu Aba and Woody, the largest of each group of islands (Chen 1993).

During the course of World War II, leaders of the allied forces began debating on where to draw lines on maps once the war came to an end. As early as May 1943, the US State Department had drawn up document

T-324 to help determine about the islands in the SCS. However, since the islands had no vital interest for any country or territory, the US position on the issue remained largely ambiguous. But it was clear that Japan should not hold on to them. Subsequent documents also made the similar argument that there was no single country that made solid claim on the islands. The US State Department document CAC-301, prepared on December 19, 1944, ahead of the Yalta Conference, recommended that the Spratly Islands be placed under the future United Nations Organization (UNO), although that would require the approval of France. Another document, CAC-308, recommended three options for the Paracel Islands: international trusteeship, a deal between France and China, and support for China's claim unless France provided an evidence of alleged transfer of the Paracel Islands to Annam by China in 1816. After the war, the US State Department realized the difficulty of placing the islands under UN control since it would require the unlikely support of France. So, the US position continued to remain unclear. After the Philippines gained independence from the US in 1946, it declared the Spratlys as part of its sphere of influence. The French also sent a minesweeper, the FR *Chevreuil*, to the Spratlys to reassert its claim over the Indochina. The French team found the Spratly Islands uninhabited on October 5, 1946, and placed a stone marker on Itu Aba Island to assert French sovereignty. On December 9, 1946, the Chinese navy sent two vessels each to the Spratlys and the Paracels. The Chinese vessels *Taiping* and *Zhongye* arrived at Itu Aba Island on December 12, 1946, and placed a rival stone marker to make its own claim of the Spratlys. And in January 1947, the French and Chinese forces landed on different islands in the Paracels and made their own claims (Hayton 2014).

During the Cold War, the superpowers – the US and the Soviet Union – were much more concerned with control over land areas than maritime ones. The US first controlled Japan and then placed it under its security protection. First, the US had unlimited access to the SCS; then at the end of the Vietnam War in 1975, the Soviet Union had unlimited access to the sea. The US naval ships navigated freely to wage war in the Indochina. But after the US withdrawal from Vietnam in 1975, the Soviet Union had unlimited access to the region through its base in Cam Ranh Bay in Vietnam without interference from either the US or China (Zha 2001). As a successor state to France, the Vietnamese government claimed the Spratly and the Paracel Islands at the San Francisco Peace Conference without being challenged by other countries. However, in January 1974, the Chinese communist forces ejected the South Vietnamese troops who were occupying the Paracels (Severino 2010). Today, Vietnam contests the claims made by China over the Spratly and Paracel Islands, stating that China had not claimed them during the 1940s. Vietnam's position is that it has held claims over the islands since the 17th century. On the other hand, the Philippines invokes its geographical proximity to the Spratly Islands as the main basis for its claim. Moreover, both the Philippines and China lay claim to the Scarborough

Shoal (known as Huangyan Island in China) – a little more than 100 miles from the Philippines and 500 miles from China.

Some recent developments

The end of Cold War, the gradual decrease of Cambodian conflicts and the improvement of situation between Vietnam with ASEAN and China were positive signs of collective security improvement in the region. But the dispute over the SCS became a hindrance to the full realization of regional security relationship. Six countries or governments – Brunei, Malaysia, the Philippines, Vietnam, China and Taiwan – claim all or part of the Spratlys or the maritime area or both. Except Brunei, all claimants have increased their troops' presence to strengthen their claims, which makes disengagement and demilitarization of the region much more difficult. The SCS disputes have broader geopolitical implications than the ownership of islands or other resources, such as oil and gas. Major shipping lanes pass near the Spratlys, two important ports of global significance – Singapore and Hong Kong – are situated close to the seas, and more than 70 percent of Japan's oil imports come through these sea lanes. While the dispute itself is considered as one major security problem for the entire Pacific region, it has the potential to create further political division and conflict among the claimant states and also security implications for countries such as Japan, the US and even Russia (Valencia 1994).

The significance of the Spratly Islands is evidenced from the evolving developments especially since the 1970s. The Spratlys cover 2.5 square miles of land spread over 250 square miles of the SCS, 50 miles away from the Philippines, 10 miles from Brunei and Malaysia, 300 miles from Vietnam, and 600 miles from China. Vietnam, China, and Taiwan claim all of the Spratlys, while the Philippines, Malaysia and Brunei have smaller claims. China displaced the South Vietnamese forces from the Paracels in 1975 and also occupied more areas in the Spratlys. In the same year, the communists that defeated South Vietnam took control of some of the islets and maintained a base on Trung Sa Island. In 1978, President Ferdinand Marcos of the Philippines declared sovereignty over the Kalaya, which included the Spratlys, and stationed 1,000 marines on the islands. In 1979, Malaysia declared sovereignty over a portion of the Spratlys as part of its continental shelf. Taiwan maintains a base on Taiping Island. Although Brunei is the only claimant state which does not maintain military force on the islands, it established an EEZ in 1993 which included the Louisa Reef. And in 1988, China and Vietnam fought a naval battle over the Spratlys which led to the sinking of two Vietnamese ships and the deaths of 72 Vietnamese seamen (Valencia 1994). Of the six claimant states, China and the Philippines have been most active in recent years in pursuing or reiterating their claims (Zha 2001). The Spratlys are a more complex issue, with more than 230 land formations covering an area of about 155,343 square miles. All claimants see rapid modernization, especially in the economic field. As the main protagonist, there is a huge stake for China to engage in a major military conflict because that could jeopardize its relations with other countries (Hindley and Bridge 1994).

The current round of tensions between China and the Philippines began in 2008–2009 after a tense but bloodless standoff between the two countries over the Scarborough Shoal, which then led to China gaining de facto control of it in 2012. As far as China and Vietnam are concerned, tensions heightened in May 2014 when China began drilling operations with an oil rig owned by the Chinese state-owned China National Offshore Oil Corporation, 120 nautical miles from the Vietnamese coast and 17 nautical miles from Triton Island, which is part of the disputed Paracel Islands. Since 2014, attention has shifted to China's construction and installation of military-capable infrastructure in the Spratly Islands. The pace and scale of China's island-building works have dwarfed other countries that engage in similar activities and is beginning to take on a more overtly strategic character, which includes the construction of multiple runways and port facilities.

There have been some instances of serious tensions in recent decades between Vietnam and China and between the Philippines and China. In 1988, China and Vietnam clashed in the Spratlys, with Vietnam losing about 60 sailors (BBC 2015). One other source puts the death toll at 72 (Valencia 1994). In early 2012, China and the Philippines engaged in a lengthy maritime standoff, accusing each other of intrusions in the Scarborough Shoal. In July 2012, China angered Vietnam and the Philippines when it formally created Sansha city, an administrative body with its headquarters in the Paracels which it called an overseas Chinese territory in the SCS. Unverified claims that the Chinese navy sabotaged two Vietnamese exploration operations in late 2012 led to large anti-China protests on Vietnam's streets. In January 2013, Manila said it was taking China to a UN tribunal under the auspices of the UNCLOS, to challenge China's claims. In May 2014, the introduction by China of a drilling rig into waters near the Paracel Islands led to multiple collisions between Vietnamese and Chinese ships. In April 2015, satellite images showed China building an airstrip on a reclaimed land in the Spratlys. In October 2015, the US sailed a guided-missile destroyer within 12 nautical miles of the artificial islands – the first in a series of actions planned to assert freedom of navigation in the region. China warned that the US should "not act blindly or make trouble out of nothing" (BBC 2015).

Efforts toward solution

The SCS dispute is undoubtedly complicated by the competing or overlapping claims by several littoral states. It is made complicated even more so by the fact that other members of the international community are either involved or have interests on the issue, which further raises the security and military stakes. ASEAN has been involved in conflict management, but it has been unable to help resolve the dispute. Despite the difficulties and challenges, there have been activities and efforts to resolve the dispute at international, regional and bilateral levels.

International level

Over the years, the Security Council (SC), which is the most powerful body of the UN, has not intervened despite the danger the SCS poses to international security. But this is not surprising for the simple reason that China, which is a veto-wielding power in the SC, is a major claimant in the SCS disputes. The ICJ, an organ of the UN, has been involved in similar issues in Southeast Asia, such as the sovereignty dispute between Indonesia and Malaysia over Pulau Ligitan and Pulau Sipadan Islands in 2002, another sovereignty dispute between Indonesia and Malaysia over Pedra Branca/ Pulau Batu Puteh islets in 2002, and a sovereignty dispute between Malaysia and Singapore over Middle Rocks and South Ledge in 2008. But the ICJ has not been involved in the SCS, which is a bigger problem. Obviously, this is because China has not consented to the ICJ's intervention and adjudication. Unsurprisingly, China refused when the Philippines sought an ICJ intervention. Similarly, the UNCLOS has been ineffective, partly because it does not have an enforcement mechanism and also does not address sovereignty issues. Moreover, in August 2006, China declared to the UN secretary-general that it would not accept any international court or arbitration with regard to disputes over sea delimitation, territorial disputes and military activities. And in July 2011, China rejected when the Philippines suggested an arbitration from ITLOS, an independent judicial body set up by the UNCLOS. The limitation of the UN was also evident in 2009 when countries were asked to submit their continental shelf delimitation applications to the UN Convention on the Limits of the Continental Shelf (CLCS). For example, a joint Vietnam-Malaysia submission was criticized by China and the Philippines. The CLCS could not consider the submissions because of the conflicting claims (Scott 2012).

Regional level

Two regional approaches have been pursued: track-2 diplomacy at the non-governmental level and track-1 diplomacy involving ASEAN and ASEAN-China at the intergovernmental level. Elite interactions through track-2 diplomacy and personal networks have been important for peace building and in preventing conflict in the SCS. Environmental issues, such as marine biodiversity protection has been a good agenda for discussions through track-2 diplomacy. One major track-2 discussion has been the Indonesia-sponsored Workshops on Managing Potential Conflicts in the South China Sea initiated by international law of the sea expert and former Ambassador

Hasjim Djalal in 1990, which included Technical Working Groups and Group of Experts Meetings focusing on issues such as environmental projects on ecosystem monitoring, biodiversity, sea level and tide monitoring as well as maritime issues including safety of navigation, shipping and communication. Other workshops and conferences included the Singapore-based S. Rajaratnam School of International Studies at Nanyang Technological University in 2007 and 2009, as well as the conference organized by the Institute of Ocean and Earth Sciences in Kuala Lumpur in November 2008 under the theme "The South China Sea: Sustaining Ocean Productivities, Maritime Communities, and the Climate." China also organized the 5th International Workshop on the Marine Environmental Change of the South China Sea in Guangzhou in November 2009 and the International Conference on Cooperation in Dealing with Non-traditional Security Issues in the South China Sea at Haikou, Hainan Province in May 2010. Similarly, the Diplomatic Academy of Vietnam and the Vietnam Lawyers Association initiated the International Workshop on the South China Sea: Cooperation for Regional Security and Development in November 2009, 2010 and 2011. However, these initiatives have not yielded a solution to the SCS disputes. Some formal discussions have also been initiated by ASEAN under track-1 diplomacy, including the 1992 ASEAN declaration on the SCS, but those

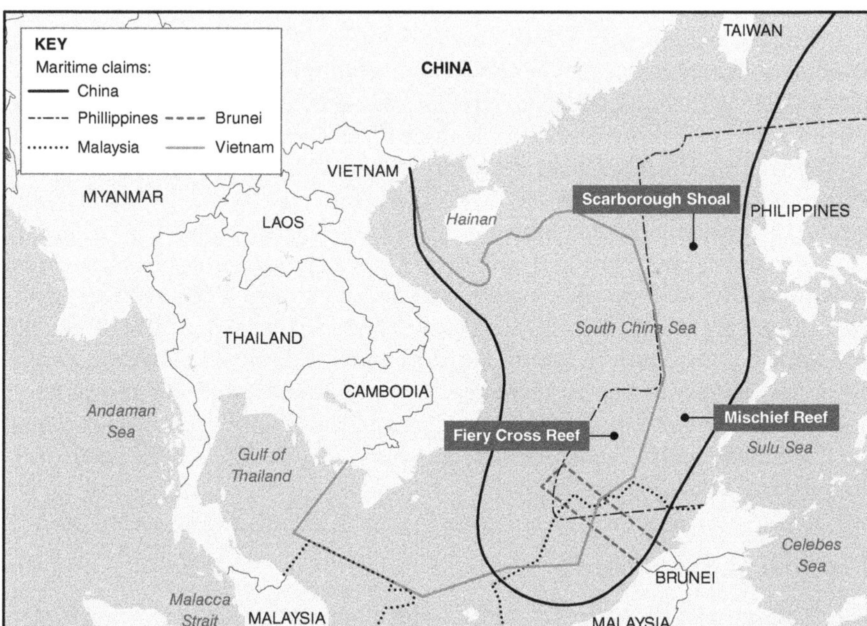

Figure 1.1 Overlapping claims and maritime flashpoint in the South China Sea

Source: Trish McAlaster, *The Globe and Mail*, accessed July 17, 2018, from www.theglobeandmail.com/news/world/tension-rising-in-south-china-sea/article24440836/.

initiatives helped only in short-term conflict prevention rather than long-term conflict resolution (Scott 2012).

Bilateral level

Apart from the international and regional levels, there have been some bilateral activities, particularly between the three most vocal claimants in the SCS disputes – China, Vietnam and the Philippines. China-Vietnam relations deteriorated following the military conflict along their land frontier in 1979. But the relation was relatively normalized again after the two countries reached a number of agreements: the land border treaty of 1999; the agreement on the demarcation of waters, EEZ and continental shelves in the Gulf of Tonkin in 2000; and the agreement on fishing cooperation in the Gulf of Tonkin in 2004. While the disputes on land border and the Gulf of Tonkin waters have been stabilized, the dispute in the SCS remains a highly contested issue between the two communist neighbors. Vietnam's claims are the second largest in the SCS after China. Vietnam claims not only a continental shelf and the 200 nautical miles of the EEZ but also the historical claims over the Spratlys and the Paracels. After many years of confrontations and statements, an Agreement on Fundamental Principles to Guide the Settlement of Sea Disputes was signed in October 2011.

Another vocal claimant in the SCS is the Philippines, which has large areas of contested claims with China in the Spratlys. Over the years, incidents of confrontation between China and the Philippines have been observed, particularly at Mischief Reef in the Spratlys and Scarborough Reef, a disputed rocky atoll about 124 miles west of Luzon, the main Philippine island. Following the ASEAN-China declaration of 2002, an Agreement for Joint Marine Seismic Undertaking in Certain Areas in the South China Sea was signed in September 2004 between the Philippine National Oil Company (PNOC) and China National Offshore Oil Corporation (CNOOC). Then in March 2005, a Tripartite Agreement for Joint Marine Seismic Undertaking in the Agreement Area in the South China Sea was signed between the PNOC, CNOOC, and Vietnam's Petro Vietnam. Discussions on joint exploration to joint development were held between China and the Philippines in 2007, but they were inconclusive. Moreover, the Philippines did not renew the 2005 tripartite agreement when it expired in July 2008 amid deteriorating bilateral relations (Scott 2012).

The lingering challenges

There are no easy answers to the SCS disputes. At the same time, it is well understood by the parties concerned as well as the international community that the disputes need to be resolved. Because of the capital spent on island-building works, the sea's rich natural resources and the revenues generated annually from the sea routes, none of the disputing parties is likely to sacrifice or surrender its claims easily. Each year, about $5.3 trillion of trade passes through the SCS, with the US trade alone accounting for $1.2 trillion (Glaser 2015a). While the tension is simmering and there is no peaceful solution in sight in the near future, the non-claimant countries want the SCS to remain international waters where there is freedom of navigation. The underlying problem is the claim of overlapping areas by countries including Brunei, China, Vietnam, the Philippines, Taiwan and Malaysia. China and Vietnam both claim sovereignty over the Paracels in the northwestern SCS. The five littoral states – Brunei, China, Malaysia, the Philippines and Vietnam – claim some or all features in the Spratlys in the southern part of the SCS. Though Taiwan is also a party to the dispute, its claims are more or less analogous to China. Both Taiwan and China claim ownership of the Pratas Islands, which are occupied by Taiwan over the Macclesfield Bank and Scarborough Shoal, the latter of which is also claimed by the Philippines (Schofield and Storey 2009). The contested claims are also reflected in the variety of names used for the islands and the sea. For example, the Chinese call the southern sea Nan Hai; the eastern sea is called Bien Dong by Vietnam; and the west Philippines sea is called Dagat Kanlurang Pilipinas by the Philippines (Scott 2012).

China and Vietnam have claimed the entire area, and others claim contiguous zones. The uncertainty in sovereignty jurisdiction has hampered or at least delayed the exploration and exploitation of natural resources, including hydrocarbons and fish. Due to the complexity of the issue, all efforts to resolve the dispute have remained largely futile. One important reason why an agreeable solution on the dispute has not materialized is that China and Vietnam have refused to give up their formal claims to the entire area. Proposals to address the dispute through multilateral forums have also not yielded any significant positive results thus far. The search for new sources of energy has entailed the urgency to address the dispute. The claimants are now interested in exploiting the resources of the sea in the areas of their respective control and even beyond. The more concerning development in recent years has been the building of artificial or man-made islands, particularly by China. The complexity of the problem has been more significant following the arbitral ruling at the PCA at The Hague in July 2016.

Fundamental problems of the South China Sea

Following the presentation of the historical and lingering problems of the SCS disputes, this section focuses on the fundamental issues of the SCS disputes based on the author's field-based research notes. The nature of complexity is that even experts or knowledgeable people on the subject matter have varying perspectives on the core issue of the dispute. The fundamental problem revolves around three major issues: territorial or sovereignty, maritime and geopolitics. The sovereignty or territorial disputes comprise two major disputes and other minor ones. The dispute over the Paracels is between China, Vietnam and Taiwan. In the Spratlys, six parties are claiming part or all of its features. There is also the Scarborough Shoal dispute between China and the Philippines. The maritime issues involve disputes over resources such as fish, oil and gas. On the question of territorial and maritime disputes, Tavares said the problem is about the logic of the claims itself. For example, on what basis do the claimants make their claims? What is the reason for them to claim those features? Is it because their sailors and ships have navigated through the surrounding seas? Does this give them rights to own those features? So, it is not clear what the basis of their claims are, or how one's claim is more justifiable than the others (Interview on January 20, 2018). The geopolitics involve power rivalry, especially between China, the US and Japan. For Hiep, this power rivalry or competition "has something to do with peace and security issues of the Asia Pacific" (Interview on December 22, 2017).

Chaturvedy said that nobody in the region likes to comment on the territorial dispute between China and other claimant states because that would create troubled relations with China. Beijing does not want any country to interfere in what it considers a bilateral issue. Since China is "powerful economically and militarily, no one wants to challenge that view" and "geopolitically the region is important because the US and EU close their economies to others" and "China fills the gap in terms of security as well" (Interview on December 21, 2017). Wisnu, however, said that the dispute is not just a territorial issue but a changing landscape of power or interest in the region which makes people act differently. She said that what had happened in the 1990s is different now. In the 1990s, it was purely about making sure that people respect each other's boundaries. There were no obvious threats and ASEAN was not as it is today. Now in 2018, ASEAN is more legally bound together. Taiwan sees ASEAN claimant states differently; China sees differently; and ASEAN sees them differently as well (Interview on January 22, 2018). Encomienda was of the view that the US and China are locked in strategic competition in the pursuit of their respective national interests. China, which is the rising regional power, is asserting its economic and political influence while the US is the status quo extra-regional power. For Encomienda, the SCS dispute is a "strategic/geopolitical rivalry between the US and China for greater influence and control of the region. The US fought in Vietnam, lost the war, and is now looking to the Philippines for control of the Southeast Asia region" (Interview on December 1, 2017). Amador believed that China attempts to "dislodge US from its hegemony in the region," while the other claimant states "always look toward the US for support and influence" (Interview on December 7, 2017).

From the Philippines perspective, Batongbacal, who is one of the leading experts in the country on the issue, said that the dispute is "primarily about resources," and all other issues such as legal, geopolitics and military are secondary. He said that for governments it is about petroleum, but for the people it is about fisheries. The Philippines need to explore and exploit the waters for its national development, so it pushes for peaceful resolution of the dispute. He said most incidents that have increased tensions are related to the fisheries issue. He further said that previous and current Philippine governments "have not paid enough attention to the fisheries issues, and instead focus on legal and political aspects" (Interview on November 30, 2017). According to Djalal, who was heavily involved in track-2 discussions on the SCS disputes, with the rise of China, other countries – particularly the US – are concerned, and therefore, call for freedom of navigation and overflight (Interview on January 19, 2018). From the US perspective, Tran said the fundamental issues are ensuring peace and upholding freedom of navigation and freedom of seas, and upholding international law, not just by the US but all members of the international community (Interview on January 26, 2018). Similar to the US perspective, the EU believes that the fundamental issues of the SCS disputes are security, freedom of navigation and peaceful settlement of the dispute as well as the respect for international law, including the UNCLOS (Interview on January 16, 2018).

Conclusion

The SCS dispute has its roots in precolonial and colonial times to the decolonization period and the Cold War era, and then to the more recent developments. While the intractable dispute remains, there have been several efforts to resolve the issue bilaterally, at the regional level and internationally or multilaterally. Over the years, the dispute has been complicated by the exertion of competing or overlapping claims by several littoral states. It has become even more complicated by the fact that other members of the international community are either involved or have interests on the issue, making security and military stakes higher. ASEAN has engaged in conflict management with China, but both sides have been unable to find an amicable solution.

2 China's claim and activities

According to Asia Maritime Transparency Initiative, a regularly updated source for information, analysis, and policy exchange on maritime security issues in Asia, China has seven outposts in the Spratlys and 20 in the Paracels. The outposts in the Spratly Islands are Cuarteron Reef, Fiery Cross Reef, Gaven Reefs, Hughes Reef, Johnson Reef, Mischief Reef and Subi Reef. The outposts in the Paracels are Antelope Reef, Bombay Reef, Drummond Island, Duncan Islands, Lincoln Island, Middle Island, Money Island, North Island, North Reef, Observation Bank, Pattle Island, Quanfu Island, Robert Island, South Island, South Sand, Tree Island, Triton Island, West Sand, Woody Island and Yagong Island. It also controls the Scarborough Shoal, which it seized in 2012. Since 2013, China has engaged in extensive dredging and artificial island building which has resulted in the creation of 3,200 acres of new land in the Spratlys and a substantial presence in the Paracels (Asia Maritime Transparency Initiative 2018a).

China's historical claims

China uses folklore, myths and legends as well as history to support its territorial and maritime claims. Chinese textbooks have been promoting the notion of the Middle Kingdom as the oldest and most advanced civilization which was situated in the middle of the universe, and surrounded by other lesser advanced states in East and Southeast Asia; and therefore, these should pay China their respect. Chinese history has deliberately not made any distinction between what was no more than hegemonic influence, tributary relationships, suzerainty and actual control. In pursuing its nationalistic goal, China has placed high importance on its history in its diplomatic efforts and on achieving their foreign policy objectives. Malik writes that China's claims in the SCS and that of Taiwan are based on the grounds that they were part of the ancient Manchu empire. China has had the tendency to treat any territory it captured at any point of time in history as their own. Moreover, the scholar believes that the writing and rewriting of history from a "nationalistic perspective to promote national unity and regime legitimacy has been accorded the highest priority by China's rulers, both Nationalists and Communists" and that the Chinese Communist Party leadership "consciously conducts itself as the heir to China's imperial legacy, often employing the symbolism and rhetoric of empire" (Malik 2013, 85–86).

According to one other scholar, the claims of islands in the SCS by PRC and ROC are based on eight facts dating from 1946 to 1949: (1) civilian and military officials were sent to formally recover the archipelagoes; (2) administrative organs were established and permanent garrisons deployed in the Paracels and the Spratlys; (3) stone tablets were erected on several islands in an official ceremony; (4) a map of the area with a U-shaped dotted line drawn around the SCS was published in 1948; (5) a new and detailed list of the names of every insular and archipelagic formation in the SCS was published the same year; (6) James Shoal (Zengmu Ansha in Chinese, at 4 degrees north latitude) was again recognized by the ROC government as the southernmost point of China's national territory, as it had been proclaimed in 1935; (7) meteorological stations were established in both the Paracels and the Spratlys and internationally recognized; and (8) Chinese nationals continued and increased their economic activities in the area (Granados 2006).

China's public claim to sovereignty over the Paracel and Spratly Islands in the SCS started as early as 1950, when the Chinese leadership reportedly denounced the Philippines President Quirino's statement that the occupation of the Spratly Islands "by an enemy" would be detrimental to the Philippines' security. Beijing said in response, "[The] People's Republic of China will never allow the Nansha Islands or any other land which belongs to China, to be encroached by any foreign power" (Lo 1989, 27). In the SCS disputes, China claims territorial sovereignty over two groups of islands and maritime rights over related waters, which is primarily based on the official statement of Zhou Enlai that was issued in August 1951 during the allied powers' peace treaty negotiations with Japan (Fravel 2011). At the San Francisco peace conference, Zhou Enlai, in his role as the Chinese foreign minister said,

> The Draft Treaty stipulated that Japan should renounce all rights to Nan Wai (Spratly) Island and Si Sha Islands (Paracels), but again deliberately makes no mention of the problem of restoring sovereignty over them. As a matter of fact, just like all the Nan Sha Islands (Spratlys), Chung Sha Islands (Macclesfield Bank) and Tung Sha Islands (Pratas), Si Sha Islands and Nan Wei Island have always been China's territory.
> (Lo 1989, 27–28)

In 1956, the Chinese government reaffirmed its sovereignty over the Spratly Islands. After the Philippine Foreign Minister Carlos Garcia made a general comment at a press conference on May 19, 1956, that some of the islands should belong to the Philippines because of their proximity, the Chinese foreign affairs ministry responded on May 26, saying:

> Taiping Island (Itu Aba) and Nanwei Island in the South China Sea together with the small islands in their vicinity, are known in aggregate as the Nansha Islands. These islands have always been a part of Chinese territory. The People's Republic of China has indisputable, legitimate sovereignty over the islands. . . . The pretext put forth by the Philippine Government to cover its attempt to invade and occupy China's territory, the Nansha Islands, is utterly untenable.
>
> (Lo 1989, 29)

A couple of years later, in March 1959, when 82 Chinese fishermen were arrested by the South Vietnamese troops in the Crescent Group, the Chinese foreign affairs ministry said the South Vietnamese navy had violated China's territorial integrity and sovereignty to reaffirm its claim over the Paracel Islands (Lo 1989).

As early as the 1970s, when the role of UNCLOS was inconclusive, the SCS had already been a trouble spot. And Chinese claims to the resources in the SCS have been backed by the willingness to use force for others to recognize its rights (Gallagher 1994). For example, in January 1974, China and then South Vietnam clashed over the Paracel Islands, which resulted in Chinese control of the area. Subsequently in May 1977, Vietnam claimed 12 nautical miles of territorial waters, 12 nautical miles of contiguous zone and a further 200 nautical miles as an EEZ, which have overlapping areas with other claimants. One most significant development of the time was the clash between China and Vietnam in March 1988 over the Spratly Islands, which led to China taking control of six islands (Guan 2000). In other words, China claims everything, including land and sea, within the Nine-Dash Line area over which it exercises sovereignty. The claimed sovereignty areas account for about 70–75 percent of the SCS. The Nine-Dash Line has its origin in ancient Xia and Han dynasty records and a map produced in 1947, known as the Eleven-Dash Line. In 1953, two dashes were removed from the Eleven-Dash Line to give the current Nine-Dash Line (Kingdon 2015). The Chinese claim of a historic right is seriously undermined by the claims of overlapping areas by the Philippines, Vietnam, Malaysia, Brunei and Indonesia as well as the parallel claim made by Taiwan. Despite the competing demands, the 1998 Law of the People's Republic of China on the EEZ and continental shelf claims EEZ in all Chinese territory as specified in the 1992 territorial sea law, which includes all the island groups in the SCS (Dutton 2011).

Both China and Vietnam claim the sovereignty of the Paracel Islands based on historical grounds. China claims that it was the first country to discover, develop, exploit and exercise jurisdiction over the Paracels, dating back to as early as the eastern Han dynasty (around 23–220 AD). Evidence from China seems to suggest that it knew some of the islands in the SCS since ancient times and started to make its claim over the Paracels in 1909. China has occupied the Paracel Islands since 1974 after taking them over from South Vietnam. China maintains that there is no dispute over sovereignty in the Paracel Islands and has refused to budge. Vietnam, on the other hand, while affirming its sovereignty over these islands, is willing to engage in negotiation on the issue. Most features in the Paracels are small, except for some low-tide elevations and submerged banks. The largest features are Woody Island, which is about 0.8 square miles; Lincoln Island, which is 0.6 square miles; Triton Island, which is 0.5 square miles; and Pattle Island, which is 0.1 square miles (Dang 2014). In May 2014, China moved nearly US$1 billion deep-sea mega oil rig Hai Yang Shi You-981 to about 17 nautical miles from Triton Island, which is about 120 nautical miles from Vietnam's Ly Son Island and about 180 nautical miles from China's Hainan Island. The seriousness of the issue was evident from the fact that Vietnam dispatched about 30 vessels from its two maritime enforcement agencies: the coast guard and the fisheries surveillance force. China also dispatched 80 vessels, including the coast guard, People's Liberation Army (PLA) navy military, and aircraft to protect the oil rig. There have been confrontations in the area on a regular basis in the form of ships chasing, running into each other, colliding, ramming and firing water cannons (Dang 2014).

China's delaying strategy

As one scholar rightly says, the puzzle in understanding the SCS issue is the problem of understanding or trying to understand Beijing's strategy. And it appears that the ambiguity is intentionally designed and woven into Chinese politics and policies (Goldstein 2011). China made a gradual expansion in the SCS during the 1970s and 1980s in a number of ways: military buildup, establishment of administrative and logistical networks, and military exercises and clashes as well as through diplomatic channels. The more important and visible initiative was the construction of physical bases. The assertion of Chinese authority began in 1970 when the People's Liberation Army Navy (PLA-N) began survey operations in the Paracels and their subsequent control by the military (Garver 1992). No other state attracts more attention than China in the SCS disputes due to its expansive claim, its use of force over the islands in the past and its growing naval capabilities. Since the mid-1990s, the Chinese have largely imposed delaying tactics on the SCS disputes. The reason behind this strategy is to consolidate its claim on maritime rights and to deter other states from consolidating their own claims. Since the mid-2000s, China has increased efforts to consolidate its position through diplomatic, administrative and military means. While China imposes itself on the issue, it also destabilizes the region. The Chinese delaying tactics, without resorting to major armed conflicts, also prevent the escalation of tensions in the SCS (Fravel 2011).

With the introduction of the open-door policy in 1978, the Chinese government made modernization of its economy a national priority. In order to achieve its goal, China needed friendly and peaceful neighbors. Since the 1980s, Beijing decided to focus on economic cooperation with other countries. Despite the new approach toward other countries, China considered certain issues such as its sovereignty claim over Hong Kong, Macau, Taiwan and the SCS non-negotiable and part of its historical territory. Because of its claims in the SCS, particularly sovereignty over the Spratly Islands, China's relationship with ASEAN has not been cordial. Though only four countries – Brunei, Malaysia, the Philippines and Vietnam – are active claimants in the SCS, the issue has an impact on the stability of the entire Southeast Asia. To advance its strategic goal, China pursued a policy of gradual increase in physical presence in the SCS without using military force from 1995 to 1998. To achieve their objective, China employed two specific strategies. The first was through diplomacy in which China said it was open to negotiation on the sovereignty of islands in the SCS. At the same time, it was prepared to shelve the sovereignty issue and work toward a peaceful solution through international law, or explore the possibility of jointly developing the resources with other claimants. Through this strategy, China participated in bilateral and multilateral negotiations, including the Indonesia-sponsored workshops on the SCS; China also declared that it will respect the UNCLOS. The second strategy was setting up territorial markers in the sea and seizing unoccupied reefs and building structures on them. The Chinese would then use those markers and structures as a basis to make its claim. To consolidate their claims, China constructed facilities that could house military personnel as well as naval vessels – first small huts on stilts, then bunkers, and eventually a large brick fortress capable of accommodating more than 50 people (Storey 1999).

While China remains a threat to other smaller nations involved in the disputes due to its enormous economic and military powers, the country is cautiously treading so as to avoid any major offensive attacks. The competing claims in the SCS became increasingly significant following China's ratification of the UNCLOS in 1996. By pursuing delaying tactics, China has emphasized strengthening its maritime rights over the disputed waters and at the same time deterring others from strengthening their own claims (Kipgen 2018). China has used diplomacy as a means to protect and promote its commercial activities. When Vietnam increased its offshore petroleum industry in collaboration with foreign oil companies in the mid-2000s, China issued 18 diplomatic objections to foreign companies involved in exploration and developmental projects between 2006 and 2007 alone. Chinese fishery vessels often detained foreign fishing boats and their crews in the disputed waters. The display of naval capabilities in patrols and training exercises by the PLA-N is one method used to deter others from challenging China's own claims (Fravel 2011).

While China's uncompromising attitude is widely considered to be an obstacle to a peaceful solution, it has also taken a step to mitigate the tensions in the SCS. It is important for any country to have peaceful borders so that it can use its resources for economic development and not for the maintenance of armies and border defense systems. This is one reason why China has avoided major conflicts with other claimants over the Spratly Islands since the mid-1990s. This policy was pursued from the late 1990s until 2007, which resulted in significant progress. As a result of China's regional integration pursuit in the areas of economic, commercial and infrastructural development, China-ASEAN bilateral trade increased from $8 billion in 1991 to $106 billion in 2004 and to $231 billion in 2008, which was higher than the trade figure between ASEAN and the US for the same year, which was $172 billion (Dutton 2011).

China has also supported ASEAN members in major infrastructure projects. One such project was the Nanning-Singapore economic corridor, focusing on the construction of an integrated railway transportation system linking Nanning, Hanoi, Ho Chi Minh City, Phnom Penh, Bangkok, Kuala Lumpur, and Singapore. Another project was the Greater Mekong Subregion, which links Kunming in China's Yunnan Province with Singapore via high-speed rail. The reason behind China's efforts for regional integration was to prevent the SCS disputes from escalation and also to create a favorable political condition that would help China's economic and military powers. Some Chinese believed that China's investment in the region and its policy of freezing disputes was an attempt to earn gratitude from the ASEAN countries, or to gain leverage that would lead to the abandonment of SCS by other claimants. Some Chinese also believed that by pursuing regional integration through substantial investment, China would maintain the upper hand in the SCS disputes and in return receive a greater share in the event of any settlement (Dutton 2011). As one scholar rightly puts it, the Chinese strategy in the SCS is a combination of political initiative to stake its claims and pursuing a policy of creeping occupation to the uninhabited features in the region through the use of military force. In other words, China deploys both political and military strategies to consolidate its claims (Gupta 2005).

China's assertiveness

China's assertiveness in the SCS started before 2009, which is the earliest year when the discourse on the issue began. Examples of China's assertiveness include the labeling of SCS as a Chinese core interest; the *Impeccable* incident; the submission of the Nine-Dash Line to the UN; the active defense of Chinese fishing activities, including the fishing ban and the patrols by administrative agencies; the legislative measures which strengthen the administration; the encouragement of tourism; challenging the claims of other claimant states; and the activities of PLA. China considers the issue of SCS similar to that of Tibet and Taiwan. China has consistently held the argument for decades that Chinese territory includes the Nine-Dash Line, which predates the formation of the PRC. However, the submission of the Nine-Dash Line to the UN happened on May 7, 2009, in response to submissions made by Vietnam and the common submission of Vietnam and Malaysia as required by the UNCLOS. But the intriguing part is that China has not clarified the nature of its legal claim of the Nine-Dash Line, either during its submission to the UN or thereafter. China has imposed fishing ban in the SCS since 1999 and extended it in 2009 to include all foreign ships, covering about two-thirds of all the disputed waters. China started to impose its ban more forcefully by deploying more ships in the disputed waters in 2011 and again in 2012. Beijing also demanded that foreign ships obtain permissions from Hainan Province in order to conduct fishing activities in the SCS in more than half of the disputed waters since 2014. The history of China's assertiveness in the SCS started around 2000, which was increased in 2005 and further strengthened after 2011 (Turcsányi 2018).

Chinese law enforcement vessels had their presence in the SCS since the mid-2000s, which peaked in 2009. The most aggressive incident occurred in 2005, when nine Vietnamese were killed. So, the Chinese expansion of fishing ban in 2009 can be attributed to the increased presence of Vietnamese boats. There was an increased presence of Vietnamese fishing vessels in 2008 near the Paracels. The number of enforcement vessels dropped significantly in 2010 and 2011, and there was no information about the detention of Chinese fishermen in 2011. It was the Philippines which reported that the Chinese attempted at least five times to disrupt their oil exploration surveys. China routinely reiterate its claims through the foreign ministry statements and/or through articles in the *People's Daily*, the state-run newspaper. Diplomatically, China became more assertive since 2007 in response to Vietnam's increasing activities to develop its offshore oilfields. It objected 18 times to foreign oil companies' attempts to work on Vietnamese projects. Foreign companies, such as BP and ConocoPhillips, abandoned their Vietnamese projects due to pressure from China. The Chinese authorities often threatened foreign companies that were trying to engage in the SCS with other claimant states that they may either lose their contracts in China and/or that their safety in the disputed waters could not be guaranteed. Moreover, the PLA-N became more active in the disputed waters since the 1990s when China increased its South China fleet. The PLA started conducting regular patrols in the sea in 2005, with the most violent incident occurring in 2007 when the Chinese navy sank a Vietnamese vessel and killed a fisherman. However, it was not only China which became aggressive in the region. The increasing activities of China were largely in response to the actions of Vietnam and the Philippines, which sought to strengthen their claims through legal measures (Turcsányi 2018).

Table 2.1 Alleged Chinese assertive actions before 2011

Chinese action	*Time of occurrence*	*Category of behavior*
Labeling the South China Sea as a Chinese core interest on par with Tibet and Taiwan	2010	Not relevant (misinterpreted)
The *Impeccable* incident	2009	Not relevant (it took place in an undisputed Chinese EEZ)
Submission of the Nine-Dash Line to the UN	2009	No policy change (China's long-standing position, triggered by a new external development)
The more active defense of Chinese fishing activities, including the imposition of a fishing ban	Since 2009	Policy adjustment (expansion of the scope of previous policy, a reaction to a new external development)
More frequent patrols by administrative agencies	Since 2005	Policy adjustment (reactions to a new external development, a continuing rise of China's presence)
The diplomatic pushback against other states' oil-related activities	Since 2007	Policy adjustment (reactions to a new external development in line with China's long-standing position, no shift in 2009–2010)
Increasing PLA-N activities	Since the 1990s	Policy adjustment (a continuing rise of activity, no explicit evidence of new assertive action)

Source: Turcsányi (2018, 43).

The Nine-Dash Line

The Nine-Dash Line (or the U-shaped line) is the dotted line with nine segments displayed on Chinese maps and claimed by China. But the Chinese position on the line remains ambiguous since Beijing has not given a clear explanation. The Nine-Dash Line had not been officially used by China in international arena to justify its claims. But in May 2009, China submitted a written complaint to the UN secretary-general protesting the submissions by Malaysia and Vietnam of the outer continental shelf to the Commission of the Limits of the Continental Shelf. In the protest notes, China claimed an indisputable sovereignty over the islands in the SCS and the adjacent waters. China also claimed that it has sovereign rights over the waters as well as the seabed and subsoil. Since then, the Chinese government has maintained the position. The Chinese Nine-Dash Line claim can be described broadly into three categories: claims to islands, national boundaries and historical claims. And according to China's 1998 EEZ and continental shelf law, China has emphasized the claims on the basis of historical rights. But the Chinese insistence on historical rights has also intensified the ambiguity of the Nine-Dash Line. Not only do the claimant states disagree, but there is no consensus within the academic circle on what constitutes 'historical rights'. Even within China, policy makers and people in academia have not clearly defined the relationship between historical rights and historic rights under the UNCLOS, as well as the conditionality and substance of historical rights (Wenjuan 2018).

The history of the Nine-Dash Line dates to 1947, when Chiang Kai-shek's nationalist government established the Eleven-Dash Line in the Chinese maps on the SCS, which included the Spratlys and other chains which the Kuomintang party declared sovereignty. Chiang was apparently fascinated by the Nazi concept of extended *Lebensraum* for the Chinese. Chiang himself was unable to engage in the expansionist agenda since he was constantly kept in check by the Japanese. But the cartographers of his nationalist regime drew up the U-shape of the Eleven-Dash Line in their attempt to expand the Chinese control areas in the SCS. At the end of the civil war in 1949 which was won by the Chinese Communist Party (CCP), the PRC revised and adopted a Nine-Dash Line after two dashes were removed in the Gulf of Tonkin in 1953. Since the end of World War II, China has redefined borders, remanufactured historical evidence and used necessary force to rename islands and unilaterally impose its version of history in the SCS. The Chinese adopted legislation in 1992 entitled "Law on the Territorial Waters and Their Contiguous Areas," which claimed four-fifths of the SCS. The expansive claim was followed by skirmishes with the navies of the Philippines and Vietnam throughout the 1990s (Malik 2013).

But some Chinese scholars have argued that the history of Chinese use of the SCS had started before the 3rd century AD and the sea had been known to the "Chinese fishermen and seafarers from time immemorial" (Gao and Jia 2013, 100). The early history of SCS and its islands had accounts of tributes paid to the imperial courts of various dynasties by barbarians from the southern seas. To these scholars, the Nine-Dash Line has become synonymous with a claim of sovereignty over the island groups that they believe always belonged to China. The Chinese government appointed a commission in 1935 which published a list of geographical names for islands in the SCS. Following the Cairo Declaration and the Potsdam Proclamation, China recovered the Xisha and Nansha Islands in the SCS from Japan in 1946. And in 1947, the Chinese government circulated an atlas internally where it had drawn up an Eleven-Dash Line claiming sovereignty over them. In the same year, the Chinese interior ministry published a list of 172 names for the SCS both in Chinese and English. There has also been consistent legislation in China since 1958 that has claimed that China enjoys sovereignty over the Dongsah, Nansha, Xisha, and Zhongsha, as well as other islands in the SCS. In 1959, the Hainan district established an administrative office on Yong Xing Island to administer the affairs of the Xisha, Zhongsha, and Nansha Islands, and later the office was transferred to Guangdong Province in 1969. And in 1984, the National People's Congress included it within the territorial administration of Hainan Administrative Region. Such legislative and administrative claims by China are also matched by its maps, which they believe can potentially become the maritime boundary between China and other claimant states (Gao and Jia 2013).

Instead of resolving the disputes, the U-shaped or the Nine-Dash Line has added more doubts and confusion to the SCS disputes. China first officially relied on the Nine-Dash Line map in its 2009 *notes verbales* submitted to the UN secretary-general. Beijing has not given any official explanation or clarification on the map as to whether it is to be taken as evidence to support its claim or merely as a graphical depiction of it. While it can be assumed that China claims all islands within the Nine-Dash Line, it is uncertain whether that includes the maritime claims as well. The problem is that the Nine-Dash Line does not have proper geographical coordinates. And the texts of the 2009 *notes verbales* failed to make any reference to historical rights and does not clarify the relation between the Nine-Dash Line map and the historical rights. But it appears from Chinese commentaries that the Chinese scholars attribute the Nine-Dash Line map to a historical value and that the map plays an important role in Beijing's claims in the SCS (Dupuy and Dupuy 2013).

China-ASEAN joint initiatives

In 2002, the ASEAN-China DOC agreed to invite the littoral countries to cooperate on certain marine activities. The DOC required littoral countries to cooperate in five activities: marine environmental protection; marine scientific research; safety of navigation and communication at sea; search and rescue operations; combating national crime, including but not limited to trafficking in illegal drugs, piracy and armed robbery at sea, and illegal traffic in arms. However, since it was a non-binding agreement, it did not provide the necessary security in maritime management. The reason for the failure to implement the agreement has been due to sovereignty disputes over islands and reefs in the sea and lack of agreed maritime jurisdiction. China and Vietnam are the two key players due to their competing sovereignty claims and the simmering tensions between the two countries. Vietnam's claim to all features is particularly troubling because it includes islands and reefs that are also claimed by Malaysia, the Philippines, and Brunei. The internal dispute among ASEAN members complicates the regional bloc's ability to establish a common position (Bateman 2011).

Two years after the agreement of the DOC, officials from the two sides formed a Joint Working Group (JWG) and held the first meeting in Manila, the Philippines, from August 4–5, 2005. The JWG agreed to meet twice a year to work on the recommendations of its Terms of Reference in four areas: guidelines and the action plan for the implementation of the DOC; specific cooperative activities in the SCS; a register of experts and eminent persons who may provide technical inputs, non-binding and professional views or policy recommendations to the ASEAN-China JWG; and the convening of workshops as the need arises. When ASEAN presented its guidelines for discussion, China objected to the idea that ASEAN members will continue to follow its standard practice of consulting among themselves before meeting China. The position of China was that disputes should be resolved bilaterally with the concerned country (Thayer 2011a).

China's assertiveness in the disputes placed it at the spotlight on the international stage. For example, the SCS disputes featured prominently at the ARF and at the inaugural ASEAN Defense Ministers Meeting Plus (ADMM Plus) in 2010. China, which was diplomatically isolated in those meetings, agreed to resume the JWG meetings. Subsequently, the fifth meeting was held in Kunming, China, in December 2010 and the sixth meeting in Medan, Indonesia, in April 2011. It became clear in the meetings that China was insistent on solving the SCS disputes directly with the concerned parties and not ASEAN as a group. In July 2011, ASEAN and China reached an agreement on the revised version of the guidelines for the implementation of the DOC, which underscored that the DOC was not an agreement between ASEAN as a group and China, and its implementation will contribute to the deepening of the ASEAN-China strategic partnership for peace and prosperity (Kipgen 2018).

The eight significant guidelines of the revised DOC were that the implementation of the DOC should be carried out in a step-by-step approach in line with the provisions of the DOC; the parties to the DOC will continue to promote dialogue and consultations in accordance with the spirit of the DOC; the implementation of activities or projects as provided for in the DOC should be clearly identified; the participation in the activities or projects should be carried out on a voluntary basis; initial activities to be undertaken under the ambit of the DOC should be confidence-building measures; the decision to implement concrete measures or activities of the DOC should be based on consensus among parties concerned and lead to the eventual realization of a COC; in the implementation of the agreed projects under the DOC, the services of the experts and eminent persons, if deemed necessary, will be sought to provide specific inputs on the projects concerned; and progress of the implementation of the agreed activities and projects under the DOC shall be reported annually to the ASEAN-China ministerial meeting (Thayer 2011a).

In addition to the DOC, ASEAN also worked on a COC. In January 2012, ASEAN officials discussed the draft to reach a common position before presenting it to China for discussion. Initially, China insisted that the DOC guidelines should be implemented first before discussing the COC but later changed its position and sought working with ASEAN officials in drafting the COC. However, due to differences among the ASEAN members, it was agreed that ASEAN would work on the draft on its own and communicate with China through the ASEAN chair. In July 2012, ASEAN released a six-point principle on the SCS: the full implementation of the DOC in the SCS; the guidelines for the implementation of the DOC; the early conclusion of a regional COC in the SCS; the full respect of the universally recognized principles of international law, including the 1982 UNCLOS; the continued exercise of self-restraint and non-use of force by all parties; and the peaceful resolution of disputes, in accordance with the universally recognized principles of international law, including the UNCLOS (Thayer 2013).

China's recent activities

Since 2013, China has expanded its artificial islands and reefs in the sea and also constructed runways, missile launchers, barracks and communication facilities. China has also increased its coast guard presence in the SCS. In some aerial photos taken between June and December 2017 and provided by the Philippine *Daily Inquirer* newspaper showed that China militarized the SCS by building runways, hangars, control towers, helipads and radomes as well as multistoried buildings constructed by China on reefs such as Fiery Cross, Subi, Mischief, McKennan, Johnson South, Gaven and Cuarteron. Some photos also show cargo ships and supply vessels believed to be supplying construction materials to the China-controlled islands. Following the revelation of the photos, Chen Xiangmiao, a Chinese expert from the state-run National Institute for South China Sea Studies, played down the significance of the construction and told the *Global Times* newspaper that "Civilian facility construction is the major focus of the South China Sea islands building and the portion of defence deployment is relatively small." However, another Chinese expert, Zhuang Guotu, said that "China has the right to build whatever it needs within its territory." For Guotu, China's military deployment was not for military expansion but to defend its security and interests. It was reported in December 2017 that China had built military facilities about four times the size of Buckingham Palace in the SCS (Phillips 2018).

In another show of power and strength in the second week of April 2018, the Chinese military conducted a massive military exercise in the disputed areas of the SCS, during which it also displayed for the first time the country's aircraft carrier strike group and the most advanced weaponry of the PLA. The drill, which was reviewed by President Xi Jinping, involved the *Liaoning*, type 052D destroyers, type 052C destroyers, type 071 amphibious transport dock and type 093 submarine, 48 warships, 76 aircraft and more than 10,000 sailors and soldiers, and it was called the "biggest maritime military parade since the foundation of the new China and a heroic display of the PLA Navy in the new era" by the PLA Daily. Song Zhongping, a Chinese military expert said, "China's strength in protecting its national maritime interest has grown. The Thursday parade could also serve as deterrence to maritime hegemony, making adversaries think twice before attempting to harm China's core national interests." Another Chinese naval expert, Li Jie, said the military drill was a strategic move from China as the waters in the SCS are a potential combat zone (Press Trust of India 2018b). And a few days later, on April 23, 2018, China unveiled a monument on Fiery Cross Reef on the Spratly Islands where it built one of its airstrips and other military facilities. The construction of the monument was to send a message to the world, particularly the other claimant states that China was ready and determined to protect what it considers its territory and maritime rights in the SCS (Reuters Staff 2018a). Another report published in March 2018 shows that China has constructed nearly 400 buildings on Subi Reef, which is the largest artificial island within the Spratly archipelago; this is believed to be about double the number of structures that Beijing has constructed in other larger islands of the Spratlys. China has 1,652 buildings in the SCS, which is more than the number of all other claimants combined (Chan 2018).

Despite the increasing assertiveness in the SCS through artificial buildings and installation of military structures as well as the military exercises, China has not abandoned its diplomatic efforts to work with ASEAN on the issue. In an interesting development, Singapore Foreign Minister Vivian Balakrishnan announced on August 2, 2018, that China and ASEAN, as an organization, have agreed on a single text to negotiate the COC on the SCS. The two sides have also agreed on the key modalities of future negotiations which will be based on a single draft document that will be edited and updated as and when necessary. China and ASEAN have worked on the DOC, a precursor to COC, since 2002 without much success. Negotiations on the COC began in March 2018 following the adoption of a framework in 2017. China, which has been opposing the intervention or interference of other powers, welcomed the announcement of Singapore as the 2018 ASEAN chair and as coordinator of ASEAN-China relations since 2015. In his response to the development, Chinese Foreign Minister Wang Yi said:

> We believe that without any disturbances from outside, COC negotiations will accelerate. . . . Past progress has shown that China and Asean countries have the ability to maintain peace and stability in the South China Sea, and have the wisdom to arrive at a set of regional rules of conduct that we all will observe. . . . It is like China and Asean countries building a house together. In the past, there were 11 designs from the 11 countries on how this house would look like. Now, we have laid in

place good groundwork for a single design of this house, and we have also put in place the fundamentals, like the supporting pillars of this house.

(Yong 2018)

The challenges

In recent years, rising oil prices in the international market and China's appetite for energy for its large population have stimulated greater interest in the exploitation of oil reserves in the SCS (Buszynski and Sazlan 2007). Some of the most important issues hindering the implementation of the DOC thereby preventing a peaceful resolution of the SCS disputes are the competing claims to features in all the sea by China, Taiwan and Vietnam. Some other challenges include growing competition for resources, the desire for claimant countries to see maritime boundaries as fences in the sea, division among ASEAN members, and militarization of the disputes (Bateman 2011). Despite the challenges, there have been efforts to reach an amicable agreement on the disputes. The agreement between China and ASEAN in July 2011 was an indication of preventing further escalation of tensions between China and Vietnam. ASEAN and China have held several talks over the years on the guidelines, particularly on the question of whether ASEAN should participate as a group or not. Vietnam has been adamant about the inclusion of an ASEAN-inclusive provision (Fravel 2011). According to the DOC, the parties in dispute agreed to resolve their territorial and jurisdictional disputes by peaceful means and not to resort to threat or the use of force (Kingdon 2015).

One contestation by China has been the notion of achieving a solution through arbitration under Annex VII of the UNCLOS, which would likely benefit members of ASEAN. Under such a situation, ASEAN would be able to present a united front against China with the condition that maritime claims must be settled under UNCLOS. In January 2013, the Philippines, a member of ASEAN, filed a case against China for alleged violation of international law over its territorial claims following over a decade of bilateral and multilateral negotiations. China refused to take part in the PCA process, making it the first country to refuse to take part in interstate disputes under UNCLOS. In March 2014, the Philippines submitted a formal case to the arbitration tribunal judges, which was an arbitral body (Kingdon 2015).

The important issue about the maritime claims under the UNCLOS is to ignore what China considers as its historical rights in the SCS while giving littoral states control over the resources that China thinks it has the right to access. China's claim of rights is largely due to the outcome of the San Francisco Conference of September 1951, which failed to identify the owner of the islands when they were dispossessed from Japan. On the other hand, Vietnam's historical claim is based on its contact with the islands during the Nguyen dynasty from the 16th to the 19th centuries. The efforts to bring a peaceful solution should aim at convincing China to compromise on its territorial and maritime claims so that other claimants can also share the benefits of resources. The hope of ASEAN members that the disputes would be resolved through multilateral negotiations in ARF has been resisted by China (Buszynski and Sazlan 2007). Although China claims sovereignty over the SCS, it is unable to exercise control over all the resources. ASEAN has depended on the presence of the US to balance the influence of China. Though this strategy seems to work, it is not effective enough to resolve the disputes (Guan 2000).

What precisely is China's claim?

There has been much discussion on the claim and position of China as well as its increasing assertiveness in the SCS. But there remain ambiguity and doubts regarding China's territorial and sovereignty claims, particularly over the Nine-Dash Line claim. After several decades of lingering tension, many analysts and policy makers still struggle to understand what precisely is China's claim in the SCS. Several experts and stakeholders alike are trying to understand the motive of China's maneuvers. Some say that Beijing claims everything within the Nine-Dash Line, whereas some others say the basis of China's claims are unclear. For example, Hongzhou said, China claims historical rights as well as economic rights within the Nine-Dash Line, including oil and gas resources. China's position on the Nine-Dash Line is that the specific details will have to be agreed upon during bilateral negotiation as a starting point for negotiation and compromise (Interview on December 20, 2017). In a different interpretation of China's claim and position, Tseng said, this is a puzzle. First, China claims territorial sovereignty of land features, such as rocks, islands, shoals and so forth. Second, China is willing to respect the 200 EEZ but vaguely mentions whether that is based on an individual island or a group of islands. China's Nine-Dash Line claims covers about 60 to 80 percent of the entire SCS. And nobody, including the Chinese themselves, really knows the details of the Nine-Dash Line claim, and China is not in a hurry to define it, which according to the Western world is the Chinese way (Interview on December 19, 2017). Along similar line, Hiep said, we don't know because they have not made clear explanations on the issue, but it seems they want to claim sovereignty over water and features – rocks and islands – within the Nine-Dash Line (Interview on December 22, 2017).

Djalal questioned the basis of the Chinese claim and said, I have asked the same question to China many times but they don't officially explain. And gradually it seems that China is claiming all the features within the Nine-Dash Line and all their maritime rights. But when you try to explain them there are more problems such as rocks, islands, seabed, reefs and so forth. Then what is the basis and what rights are they talking about. Under the UNCLOS, rocks cannot have EEZ. There is a difference between rocks and islands. China argues that they have islands. According to UNCLOS, islands should have lands and other features that could survive human habitation. If they cannot sustain human habitation, they cannot be called islands. People can go there and spend holidays by taking necessary foods, but that is not sustained by the natural resources on the features (Interview on January 19, 2018). Agusman said, China claims all features within the Nine-Dash Line but they don't openly explain or provide a good basis for such claim. What they claim is a strategic comfort zone. They cannot even reconcile with international law because this is very political and domestic. This is about China's traditional thinking. The issue also has to do with preserving the leadership of the CCP (Interview on January 23, 2018). Batongbacal said China has not specified its claim, so it is difficult to understand. However, the 2016 arbitral award deems it to be a claim to living and non-living marine resources within the area enclosed by the Nine-Dash Line (Interview on November 30, 2017). And Amador said it is the Nine-Dash Line, but nobody knows what exactly it is because no one can exercise unilateral control over international waters. We must follow UNCLOS on water disputes as it is the only international law organization that deals with water disputes. Nobody recognizes the Nine-Dash Line except China. The Philippines brought the case to the PCA precisely to understand the claims of China (Interview on December 7, 2017).

Why is China not forcibly occupying the South China Sea?

Another piece of the puzzle is that given its unparalleled military and economic powers, why is China not forcibly occupying the SCS? Though it seems a straightforward answer, experts and several stakeholders have different views on the issue. For example, Hikmahanto said, under international law, use of force is permitted under two instances. First, under Article 51 of the UN Charter, there is the right to defense if a country comes under attack. Second, it is mandated by the UN Security Council (UNSC) under Chapter VII of the UN Charter. If China uses force to forcibly occupy the SCS, the international community will not accept it. Using force to gain territory is not recognized by international law or by the international community. It is not necessary for China to use force to control or expand its presence in the SCS. China needs the world to do business with and to feed its population of over one billion. Similarly, the world needs China. China has become more civilized and it will use a civilized way to approach this issue through their diplomats and scholars, and write articles in local newspapers to explain their position. China is not like North Korea which does not need diplomacy or scholars to advance their goals (Interview on January 18, 2018). Taking a different perspective, Arif said that China is trying to do so, but no country can afford war or open conflict at the moment including China. What China can do or has been doing is what we call salami slicing, that is, gradually building or expanding its presence; it will eventually say to others to maintain the status quo by the time they will already have extensive control. China is using a threat of force – if not already actually using it – against other claimant states. It is not in the interest of China to go to war, and it is not the way China behaves. China is happy to be working on certain issues for decades or even a hundred years. It is not Chinese strategic culture to settle issues immediately, like some Western countries do (Interview on January 22, 2018).

Pattiradjawane said the Chinese cannot do that. The environment of these "fake islands" is not conducive for human survival. For example, there are strong winds (of about 200–300 km/hr) and tropical storms, sands, hurricanes and a hostile environment. The environment is not friendly, and there are obstacles for China to expand its claims. Moreover, China has no capacity to dominate or control the region. If it were easy, the US would have done it during the Vietnam War (Interview on January 17, 2018). Baviera observed that if China were to do that, it would mean war, which would entail driving away both the Philippines and Vietnam's military presence in the islands. This would have a direct negative impact on China's regional initiatives, such as the Belt and Road Initiative. Suffering a political cost will impact China's economy too, which has been in a bad state lately. The region is an important market for the Chinese (Interview on December 4, 2018). Lean stated that China has the military power to do so, but the political cost will be too high if China wants to control the entire sea. It will also give enough reasons for other claimant states to invite other powers to interfere in the region or on the issue. It is not in China's interest to invite the international community and internationalize the issue. Moreover, China's own standing in Southeast Asia will be damaged. Thus, it is not in China's interest to do that (Interview on December 26, 2017).

Taking a different view from the rest, Naval argued that China has already done it in a way that it can no longer be reversed. Examples are the construction of artificial islands, land filling, reclamation and so forth. They have already positioned their weapons and structures beyond the natural state. They can send reinforcements anytime since they already have de facto military bases and have occupied those features. China will not be willing to dismantle the artificial islands and they prefer to be unfriendly later on while reaping the benefits of being quiet now (Interview on December 6, 2017). Along similar line, Guan believed that China has effectively occupied the key points in the SCS and there is no need for China to do more than what it has already accomplished (Interview on December 20, 2017). Strategically, Banlaoi believed that China is calculating its moves on the basis of other claimants. China is doing it slowly in order to avoid stronger actions from other claimants – slicing it slowly – now that it has artificial islands – a small move but a big outcome. China now establishes seven features in the Spratlys and also in the Paracels. China's strategy is to gradually control the entire area and put all other claimant states in a situation where they cannot do anything (Interview on December 5, 2017). However, considering the geopolitics, Ariadno stated that the SCS is not just about the littoral states but also other major maritime powers. China realizes that there are other big maritime powers if it decides to use force especially with regard to the enforcement of international freedom of navigation (Interview on January 25, 2018).

Belt and Road Initiative

With a view to expanding its global outreach through infrastructural development and investments, China introduced a new Silk Road strategy known as "One Belt, One Road" (OBOR), which President Xi Jinping originally announced during official visits to Indonesia and Kazakhstan in 2013. The massive plan was subsequently promoted by Premier Li Keqiang during state visits to Asia and Europe. Sensing the possibility of misinterpretation of the word "one" by the international community, China renamed it as the Belt and Road Initiative (BRI) in 2016, also with a goal to enhance regional connectivity. The project is planned for completion in 2049, which will coincide with the 100th anniversary of the People's Republic of China. The multibillion dollar initiative aims not only to develop infrastructure but also to create a large economic market by enhancing relations with nations in Central Asia, Europe, the Middle East, North Africa, Southeast Asia, and South Asia. When the specific policies of OBOR was released in 2015, it included six international economic corridors at an estimate value of US$890 billion for "One Belt (Silk Road Economic Belt) and two routes for the Maritime Silk Road. The corridors were the China-Mongolia-Russia Economic Corridor, the New Eurasia Land Bridge (Second Eurasia Land Bridge) Economic Corridor, the China-Central Asia West Asia Economic Corridor, the China-Indochina Peninsula Economic Corridor, the China-Pakistan Economic Corridor, the BCIM Economic Corridor, and the 21st Century Maritime Silk Road. The silk road will pass through the South China Sea and the Indian Ocean to Europe and Africa and routes from the South China Sea to the South Pacific. And because of its ongoing efforts in Africa and Latin America, the OBOR concept is not limited to Eurasia but becomes China's ambitious global project (Aoyama 2016).

Simultaneously with the BRI, China has introduced other strategically important initiatives such as building a strong maritime nation strategy, diplomacy of a great power with Chinese characteristics, a new vision of great power relationship between China and the US, and a new neighborhood diplomacy with amity, sincerity, mutual benefit, and inclusiveness. With these new initiatives, China has elevated its frontiers, borderlands and ocean to a level of critical importance. Consequently, management and settlement of outstanding territorial and boundary disputes with its neighbors have become even more important. China believes that with its rise in economic and military powers, the time has come to fulfill its dream of rejuvenating it as a great nation. For it to reach that potential, it understands the need for having a stable and peaceful relationship with its neighbors. The BRI, which starts with its neighborhood, aims to balance between the approaches of protecting its sovereignty, territorial integrity and maritime rights, and the ambition of becoming a strong maritime nation. China has three main types of disputes – land boundary, maritime boundary and sovereignty disputes over offshore islands. To address all these challenges, Beijing needs a peaceful international environment, the commitments from others, as well as economic, security and cultural cooperation from the countries involved. The support, commitment and cooperation from partner nations will be key to the success of China's ambition. So, the BRI is China's strategy to enhance its global presence through land and sea routes (Lingjie 2015).

But an interesting question is whether the BRI is a bold statement of China's new geopolitical strategy or an umbrella term of diverse policy initiatives. Despite the ambitious nature of the initiative, China promotes it as a vision for harmony, peace and prosperity rather than a geopolitical and/or diplomatic assertion of making an international order. For example, at a press conference in March 2015, Chinese Foreign Minister Wang Yi said China has no interest in challenging the world order established to fight against fascism, nor does it have the intention to change the international system which it has been part of. However, he said that China wants to develop a world which is more equal, harmonious and secure. Along similar line, the Chinese Vice Foreign Minister Zhang Yesui said during his speech at the China Development Forum on March 21, 2015, that "China is a participant, constructor and contributor of the current international order and system" and that "the OBOR initiative is an economic cooperation proposal, it is not a tool of geopolitics," and "it is not directed against any specific country or organization but is a useful complement to the existing international and regional institutions." The Chinese Commerce Minister Gao Huchen said the "OBOR will be based on each country's natural endowments, advocating "one country one policy" [and that] through the construction of OBOR, different and diversified countries are intertwined together, thus promoting mutual development and dependence, and regional stability" (Hong 2016, 4–5).

While China defends the peaceful purpose of the BRI, many in the international community continue to question the real intention of such ambitious initiative. It is, however, clear that certain issues have triggered Beijing's increasing effort of enhancing its global presence. This includes China's aim to get access to energy resources from other countries, to secure security along its border provinces, as well as the need for market for its goods and services. And one other aspect is China's pursuit of a new type of major power relations and/or a new model of major country relations which then Chinese Vice President Xi Jinping introduced during his visit to Washington in February 2012, and later elaborated in more details at the Sunnylands Summit with President Barack Obama in June 2013. China wants to establish its relations with the US on the principle of no conflict or conflict confrontation, mutual respect and a win-win cooperation. Beijing wants to reach a principled agreement with the US which respects China's core interests such as sovereignty, security and development, which it hopes would help set the foundation for other areas of bilateral cooperation. While China wants to achieve an equal major power status with the US, the latter has been unwilling or reluctant to recognize such overture. The failure or reluctance to recognize the rise of China has increased the Chinese nationalist pride, especially under the leadership of the Communist Party of China (Baviera 2016). The bottom line is that regardless of China's denial, the BRI is undoubtedly and partly an attempt to exert its diplomatic, economic and geostrategic influence in the international new world order which Beijing envisions to establish.

Conclusion

China uses folklore, myths and legends as well as history to support its territorial and maritime claims in the SCS. The Chinese history has deliberately not made any distinction between what was no more than hegemonic influence, tributary relationships, suzerainty and actual control. In pursuing its nationalistic goal, China has placed high importance on its history in its diplomatic efforts and to achieve its foreign policy objectives. But there remains ambiguity and doubts regarding China's territorial and sovereignty claims, particularly over the Nine-Dash Line. After several decades of lingering tensions, many analysts and policy makers still struggle to understand what precisely is China's claim in the SCS. Several experts and stakeholders alike are trying to understand the motive of China's maneuvers. Some say that Beijing claims everything within the Nine-Dash Line, whereas some others say the basis of China's claims is unclear.

But what is clear is that China has been using different methods to pursue its objectives in the SCS, including a delaying strategy and increased assertiveness. The strategy is evident from its pursuance of bilateral negotiations with the littoral states, as well as holding dialogue with ASEAN through the DOC and COC. Beijing has used the BRI to enhance its soft power and at the same time increase its presence in the SCS through naval exercises and physical installations, such as land reclamations and building artificial islands. Though China is assertive and adamant on its claims, it does not want to forcefully occupy the entire SCS for different reasons, including the possibility of other claimant states inviting other powers to interfere on the issue. Moreover, it is not in China's interest to internationalize the dispute. What China does is salami slicing, that is, gradually increasing its activities before a solution is achieved, either amicably or otherwise.

3 Other claimant states and ASEAN's challenges

Taiwan's claim and position

When the PRC was established in October 1949, it was politically divided into two parts because the government of ROC retreated to Taiwan after the civil war. Ever since, the cross-straits relations have undergone different stages. The first stage was from December 1949 to October 1971, when the PRC had not yet been admitted to the UN. There were military standoffs across the Taiwan Straits, and both the PRC and ROC claimed to the international community that they were the true Chinese representative. The second stage was from October 1971 to July 1987, when the PRC was admitted into the UN and Taiwan became isolated politically at the international forum. Under the one-China policy, countries were able to establish ties with either the PRC or the ROC but not both. Subsequently in 1975, the ROC lost its diplomatic ties with countries in Southeast Asia. By the mid-1980s, the ROC's official diplomatic missions worldwide had been reduced to only 23, but the number of representative offices in foreign countries continued to increase. As a result, the number of international representative offices had increased by 85 in 1987. The third stage was from 1987 to 1997, following the lifting of martial law in the ROC in July 1987. The civil war with the communists in mainland China ended in 1991, and subsequently governmental institutions were recognized and there were more interactions between Taiwan and China. The Asian financial crisis in 1997 marked the fourth phase of the cross-strait relations. China's economic power grew while Taiwan's remained relatively unchanged. China did not generate its own capital but it became economically strong enough to provide economic assistance to countries in the region (Ku 2017).

Taiwan (or ROC) was the first country to make sovereignty claims over the SCS – the Pratas Islands (Tungsha Islands), Macclesfield Bank (Chungsha Islands), the Paracel Islands (Shisha Islands) and the Spratly Islands – after World War II following the Japanese withdrawal from the islands. In November 1946, the ROC's interior ministry restored its sovereignty over the SCS atolls. And in December 1947, the ROC renamed the islands and formally transferred its administration from Guangdong Province to the

Hainan special region. In 1948, the ROC published an official map of the sea in a U-shaped line. However, the ROC's claim over the Spratlys and the Paracels was challenged by France in 1947 and by the Philippines in 1949, and its claim was disrupted between 1950 and 1956 because of the defeat of the Kuomintang's nationalist government, also known as Kuomintang or KMT, in the Chinese civil war. But the Kuomintang government was able to established a garrison on Itu Aba, also known as Taiping Island, in 1956, and ever since the ROC has controlled the island. In addition, the ROC also has control over Ban Than Reef or Zhongzhou Reef, which is about 5 kilometers from Itu Aba, as well as the Pratas Islands or Tungsha Islands (Hsiao and Lin 2016).

China's historical claim of the SCS originated from Taiwan. The term "historical waters" first appeared in Taiwan's government document in 1993 and almost became part of Taiwan's law but it was eventually rejected. Taiwan's policy became evident in 1988 following the arrival of the Chinese forces in the Spratlys. China occupied the Fiery Cross Reef in late 1987 and five more features in 1988. Chinese and Vietnamese forces engaged in military confrontation on March 14, 1988, after the Chinese forces landed on Johnson Reef. The military clash resulted in the death of 64 Vietnamese marines. Taiwan has effective control of one single feature in the Spratlys, that is the largest island, Itu Aba. Following the arrival of the Chinese forces, Taiwan felt the need to secure its claims. Subsequently in July 1989, the Taiwanese government asked its interior ministry to convene a committee to demarcate its territorial sea and EEZ. Again, in October 1992, an inter-ministerial task force was formed under the interior ministry to coordinate Taiwan's official policy on the SCS. At the same time, the planning department published a paper on the legal status of Taiwan's historic waters claim. In March 1993, the task force agreed upon a set of policy guidelines which was approved by the government. On August 10, 1993, the government's policy planning department explained that its historical rights claim in the SCS is based on the 1948 U-shaped line (Hayton 2018).

The consequences of the one-China policy

The one-China policy remains a delicate issue not just for the international community but within Taiwan itself. According to Beijing, the question of ROC is irrelevant since the island is part of the PRC. But for many Taiwanese and their supporters, they consider that they are occupied by illegal forces. The irony is that the ROC has existed itself as a state since its founding in 1912 and has never ceased to be a state. For many, neither the Japanese occupation nor the creation of PRC has deprived them of their right to exist as an independent state. However, over the years, the role of Taiwan as a sovereign state has diminished and the power to establish diplomatic relations with other nations has been limited. This is largely due to the fact that the PRC has pressured foreign states from establishing or maintaining ties with the ROC (Hsieh 2009). As recently as March 2018, China urged the few remaining countries that have maintained diplomatic ties with Taiwan to recognize the one-China policy and ditch Taiwan. According to China, Taiwan is a province of the PRC and has no right to establish state-to-state ties with other nations. On the sidelines of the annual meeting of parliament in Beijing, the Chinese Foreign Minister Wang Yi said, "Upholding the "one China" principle and not having official contacts with Taiwan has already become one of the international norms for countries to follow," and that "establishing diplomatic relations with the People's Republic of China, the only legal representative of the entire Chinese people, and having normal cooperation is obviously the correct choice that conforms to the times." It was very clear that Taiwan did not share the PRC's view when Chiu Chui-cheng, deputy minister of Taiwan's China policy-making Mainland Affairs Council, said "Mainland China should fully respect our rights to maintain diplomatic ties with our allies" and further stated that "during the past two years, mainland China has continued to maliciously manipulate its 'one China' policy in the international community and squeeze Taiwan's international space with its zero-sum thinking. That has hurt the feelings of the Taiwanese people" (Reuters Staff 2018b). In fact, Taiwan's international legitimacy had started facing problems when it occupied China's seat in the United Nations (UN) because of the recurrent challenges to its status posed within the organization. Such a lingering challenge was compounded in 1979 when the US revoked its diplomatic ties with Taiwan in favor of the government in Beijing, thereby revoking a critical security treaty. The subsequent passage by the US Congress of the Taiwan Relations Act for upholding a separate existence was largely symbolic, as Taipei has been denied normal or full membership in international organizations (Leifer 2001).

Taiwan's claim and position in the SCS is largely affected by China or the China factor. Despite being a claimant state, its position and claims are limited by Beijing's "One China" policy, which is adhered to by all ASEAN claimant states. In other words, the ASEAN states do not recognize Taiwan as a sovereign state. Moreover, when cross-straits relations are good, Taiwan and mainland China (or the PRC) tend to work together on a shared agenda of promoting territorial claims in the SCS. But when relations are strained, Taiwan becomes more concerned with the security threat posed by China, and therefore, pursues a more conciliatory approach toward the ASEAN claimant states to balance Beijing. But prior to the 1996 Taiwan Straits crisis, things were a little more apparent. For example, during the clash between Vietnam and the PRC at Johnson Reef in the Spratlys in 1988, Taiwan provided tacit support to the latter. Also, during the 1990s, participants from Taiwan and China cooperated at the workshops organized by Indonesia on managing potential conflicts in the SCS. But things apparently changed after the election of President Ma Ying-jeou in 2008, that is, there was little coordination between Taiwan and the PRC on the SCS. Taiwan's policy on the SCS is also dependent on the desire to improve ties with the ASEAN claimant states because of its diplomatic isolation. Moreover, Taiwan's internal party politics and bureaucratic coordination under different administrations have also played a role. President Lee Teng-hui (1988–2000) established a legal mechanism to strengthen Taiwan's legal claim on the SCS for the most part of the 1990s but took a dramatic turn in 1999 by replacing the marine forces stationed on Itu Aba with coast guard personnel. But his successor President Chen Shui-bian (2000–2008), in an attempt to strengthen Taipei's position in the SCS, ordered the construction of an airstrip on Itu Aba Island. But when President Ma Ying-jeou came to power in 2008, he emphasized an environment conducive for cross-straits energy and other functional cooperation in the SCS (Hsiao and Lin 2016).

Several cross-straits relations have impacted Taipei's policy on the SCS. For example, after the death of Chiang Kai-shek in April 1975, Chiang Ching-kuo took significant steps to relax tensions with China by permitting indirect trade and contacts with the mainland by the Taiwanese people. He was also prepared to begin negotiations with the communists after lifting the travel ban in October 1987, but he died before talks could begin (Chai 1999). Even today, the issue of cross-straits relations remains a sensitive and divisive matter between the KMT and the Democratic Progressive Party (DPP), also known as Minjindang (MJD). For example, the DPP had criticized President Ma Ying-jeou for undermining Taiwan's economic and political independence by negotiating and cooperating with mainland China on the basis of one-China policy. The DPP also criticized President Ma Ying-jeou for failing to protest against China for the latter's deployment of oil rig Hai Yang Shi You-981 (HYSY-981) in waters near the Paracels which are claimed by China, Taiwan and Vietnam. The deployment of HYSY-981 reinforced the argument that Taiwan is an integral part of China, which also led to attacks against the Taiwanese businesses during anti-China riots in Vietnam in 2014. The DPP's policy, which is evident in the National Security Chapter of the party's ten-year policy platform released in 2011, shows the DPP's policy on waters surrounding Taiwan, including the SCS. The party believes disputes and conflicts should be resolved by those countries whose interests are affected, and within a multilateral framework, and through joint development by setting aside controversies. The DPP also supports a multilateral negotiation on issues such as maritime resource development, pollution prevention, and navigation security in order to sustain the maritime resources, as well as to preserve peace and security in the sea (Hsiao and Lin 2016).

The second challenge between Taiwan and China is lack of mutual trust. The PRC's deployment of missiles which are aimed at Taiwan, and Beijing's refusal to renounce the use of force against Taipei, mean that China remains the primary security threat for Taiwan. Moreover, there is a discontent within Taiwan that they are being excluded from activities leading up to the adoption of guidelines for implementing the DOC as well as in the process of negotiating a formal COC in SCS. After ASEAN and China agreed on the DOC in 2011, Taiwan's ministry of foreign affairs released a statement reiterating its stance on the SCS, that is, safeguarding sovereignty, shelving disputes, promoting peace and reciprocity and encouraging joint exploration, and its readiness to work with relevant parties in the region to resolve the disputes, and also stated that Taiwan will not respect any resolution on the SCS without its participation (Hsiao and Lin 2016).

The other challenge is about Taipei's military cooperation with Beijing. If Taiwan maintains military cooperation with China, it risks further alienation from the ASEAN claimant states, as well as the US. In recent years, there have been growing suspicion from ASEAN states over Taipei's behavior. Not only does Taiwan have similar territorial claims with China in the SCS, but it has consistently opposed the unilateral actions of ASEAN claimant states while it has not criticized the increasing Chinese assertiveness. Taipei's dilemma has become even more so apparent in recent years as the US took a more active part in the SCS since 2010. The US has been at loggerheads with China on the questions of freedom of navigation and on what basis of international law can the maritime and territorial disputes be managed and eventually resolved. Though the US has maintained that it does not support any particular claimant state, under the Obama administration it became more vocal particularly on the issue of the Chinese claim of the Nine-Dash Line. The US also supported the Philippines over the arbitral case against China under UNCLOS and also proposed the idea of freezing all activities that could likely escalate tensions in the SCS, as well as a binding COC between ASEAN and China. Moreover, the US has strengthened its military cooperation with Vietnam and the Philippines as well as other Asian countries, which can be construed as a design to balance the rise of China in the region and its growing assertiveness in the SCS. Taiwan is in a difficult situation. If Taipei decides to side with China on the SCS, the US may reconsider its commitment to defend it in case the island comes under military threat or actual military attacks from China. However, if it decides to ally openly with the US, it could rekindle Beijing's suspicion of Taipei, which may lead to cross-straits tensions (Hsiao and Lin 2016).

The overall Taiwan policy in the SCS is to seek a peaceful solution of territorial disputes, particularly in the Spratlys. Despite its many challenges, Taiwan is willing to cooperate with other claimant states on areas such as navigation safety, pollution control, disaster relief, seaborne rescue, oceanographic research, and ecological conservation, which is in consonance with the principles of the 1992 ASEAN declaration on the SCS, which called for peaceful settlement of disputes and to explore all possibilities for cooperation on issues relating to the safety of maritime navigation and communication, protection against pollution of the marine environment, coordination of search and rescue operations, combating piracy and armed robbery and collaboration in campaign against illicit drug trafficking. After the 1995 Mischief Reef incident between the PRC and the Philippines, Taiwan echoed the position of ASEAN and the US to refrain from taking actions that could destabilize the SCS and endanger the peaceful settlement of the dispute in the Spratlys. Over the years, Taiwan has maintained five basic principles on the SCS: (1) insist on its sovereignty claim over the Spratlys; (2) support any actions to settle the dispute by peaceful means; (3) oppose any provocative move in the region that would trigger new conflict; (4) support the idea of temporarily shelving the sovereignty jointly; and (5) continue to take an active part in the workshop on managing potential conflicts in the SCS and other related international conferences and fully cooperate with other claimant states to avoid conflict (Lin 1997).

The Philippines' claim and activities

The Philippines occupies a total of nine features in the Spratlys: Commodore Reef, Flat Island, Loaita Cay, Loaita Island, Nanshan Island, Northeast Cay, Second Thomas Shoal, Thitu Island, and West York Island. Out of the nine features, Thitu is the largest island and it is the only feature which has the only Philippine airstrip in the Spratlys (Asia Maritime Transparency Initiative 2018b). The Philippines invokes its geographical proximity to the Spratly Islands as the main basis for its claim. Besides the proximity issue, the Philippines had considered that all nationals or any member of the allied powers had equal rights for exploitation and settlement of the Spratly Islands since there was no proper territorial settlement after the Japanese government had surrendered all its rights, title and claim of sovereignty over the islands at the 1951 San Francisco Conference. The Philippines considered that the "seven-island group" or internationally known as the Spratly Islands by default became the trusteeship of the victorious allied powers after the defeat of Japan. It was on this principle that the Philippines believed it had equal opportunity of freedom in the Spratly Islands, or what it called "Freedomland." Despite its claim in the Spratlys, the Philippines adopted an equivocal policy on the issue in order to avoid direct confrontation with other countries. This was evident from the fact that the Philippines did not send any troops or naval forces to the disputed islands in 1956 when two other claimants – Taiwan and South Vietnam – both sent their forces to assert their sovereignty claims over the islands. From late 1956 to the late 1960s, the Taiwanese presence in Itu Aba, the largest island of the Spratlys, was the only one where Taiwanese forces made a continuous presence in the archipelago. The South Vietnamese also sent its naval forces to set up markers and plant flags in the islands. Though China immediately protested the presence of the South Vietnamese forces, it did not send its forces, most likely because of its limitation of naval capability at the time (Lo 1989).

The root of the Philippines' claim of sovereignty over some of the Spratly Islands began during World War II, although it officially started in 1971. During the war, some of the Spratly Islands were used by the Japanese navy to support military operations in Southeast Asia. After the war, the newly independent Philippines expressed its concern that these islands may be used by hostile nations. In 1946, the Philippines foreign minister suggested that the "New Southern Islands," a term used by the Japanese to refer to all islands in the SCS, be given to the Philippines, although the minister did not make clear on what legal basis he made such claim. A few years later, in May 1950, the Philippines President Elpidio Quirino made a statement that the occupation of Spratly Islands by an enemy state would be detrimental to the Philippines' national security. The Chinese government protested the Philippines' claim and called it a propaganda statement with instructions from the US government. The claims and counterclaims between the Philippines and China did not escalate into a major issue. However, the issue gradually picked up again, and as a result on May 29, 1956, the Chinese ministry of foreign affairs issued a statement reiterating its claim of sovereignty over the Spratly Islands. The statement was made in response to a reported comment of the Philippines Vice President and Secretary of Foreign Affairs Carlos P. Garcia that the Spratly Islands should belong to the Philippines by virtue of their proximity. The Chinese protested that it was an attempt by the Philippines to invade and occupy its territory (Lo 1989).

Moreover, both the Philippines and China lay claim to the Scarborough Shoal (known as Huangyan Island in China) – a little more than 100 miles from the Philippines and 500 miles from China (Rosen 2014). The current round of tensions between China and the Philippines began in 2008–2009 after a tense but bloodless standoff between the two countries over the Scarborough Shoal, which then led to China gaining de facto control of it in 2012. The Philippines filed a case at the international tribunal at The Hague in January 2013 following a tense standoff between the Chinese and Filipino forces at Scarborough Shoal in April 2012. The case, which was brought under the arbitration provisions of UNCLOS, challenged the legality of China's claim of the Nine-Dash Line in the SCS, which according to the Philippines is against international law.

However, the Philippines apparently changed its position under Rodrigo Roa Duterte, who assumed the office of the 16th president of the Philippines on June 30, 2016. Baviera said the Duterte government has a new policy on bilateral negotiations between the Philippines and China, that is, to first calm down the tension between the two nations. A period of renewing confidence needs to be established in order to reduce military threat. Baviera believed that there were opportunities lost because of the Philippines' 2017 ASEAN chairmanship. If the Philippines had taken a radical approach, other countries could have resisted, particularly Cambodia. For ASEAN, China's participation in ASEAN+3 (China, Japan, and South Korea), the Asia-Pacific Economic Cooperation (APEC) and ARF meetings are important, especially given the fact that the Trump administration's policy on the region is uncertain and unpredictable. Baviera added that the way things are approached are different under different administrations but the fundamental interests of the Philippines remain the same, that is, security, access to resources and territorial integrity. The Philippines' approach under Duterte is focused on the economy. In fact, not just Duterte but both the Aquino and Arroyo governments also focused on the economy. When it comes to the economy, China plays an important role in the region. Bilateral ties with China are important, and an independent foreign policy is fundamental to the Duterte government (Interview on December 4, 2017). Batongbacal said the Philippines' policy on the SCS depends on who is in power. He also said that the government of Benigno Aquino III believed that ASEAN could play a role. The Aquino government thought that multilateral approach could work for dispute settlement. However, Duterte sees no role of ASEAN in the settlement of the SCS disputes (Interview on November 30, 2017).

Vietnam's claim and activities

Vietnam occupies about 49 to 51 outposts which spread across 27 features in the SCS, including facilities built on 21 rocks and reefs in the Spratly Islands. The 27 features are Alison Reef, Amboyna Cay, Barque Canada Reef, Central Reef, Collins Reef, Cornwallis South Reef, Discovery Great Reef, East Reef, Grierson Reef, Ladd Reef, Lansdowne Reef, Namyit Island, Pearson Reef, Petley Reef, Sand Cay, Sin Cowe Island, South Reef, Southwest Cay, Spratly Island, Tennent Reef, West Reef, Alexandra Bank, Grainger Bank, Prince Consort Bank, Prince of Wales Bank, Rifleman Bank and Vanguard Bank. The status of two construction projects on Cornwallis South Reef is unclear. In recent years, Vietnam has reclaimed new land at eight of the ten rocks it occupies and has built out many of its smaller outposts on submerged reefs and banks (Asia Maritime Transparency Initiative 2018c).

Vietnam's claim in the SCS overlaps with the claims of Malaysia, Indonesia, Brunei, the Philippines, China and Taiwan. Vietnam's maritime claims in the central part of the SCS or which Vietnamese call the Eastern sea (Bien Dong) are complicated by rival sovereignty claims to the Paracel Islands (east of Vietnam and southeast of Hainan) and to the many islets, reefs, and atolls which are spread out across the Spratly areas between southern Vietnam, East Malaysia, Brunei, and Palawan. Not only Vietnam but other claimant states such as Taiwan, China, the Philippines and Malaysia also maintain garrisons on some of the isles in the Spratly Islands. In the 1970s, when China seized Pattle Island in the western half of the Paracels from South Vietnam and the new Socialist Republic of Vietnam took over the South Vietnamese positions in the Spratlys, tension began between Hanoi and Beijing. The Paracel Islands, which Vietnam claims, have been effectively controlled by China since 1974. Since 1994, Vietnam and China have actively engaged in negotiations to delineate their maritime border. Subsequently, during Chinese Prime Minister Zhu Rongji's visit to Hanoi from December 1–4, 1999, the two countries reached an agreement over their maritime border in the Gulf of Tonkin. Following the agreement, the foreign ministries of the two countries signed a land border treaty on December 31, 1999. Vietnam and China have particularly claimed the Spratlys as an indispensable part of their history for a long time. Both countries perceive the sea as analogous to land, and therefore, discussion on the delimitation of maritime zones have been discussed on the same terms as those in delineating land borders (Tønnesson 2000).

Since China is its main rival as well as a major trading partner, Vietnam has taken several steps to maintain good relations with Beijing. It has pursued three basic strategies. The first strategy is through high-level party, state and military visits. Vietnam has negotiated for joint statements, agreements and treaties to avoid developments that could disrupt or complicate other areas of bilateral cooperation, especially that may harm Vietnam's national interests. High-level meetings enable the adoption of guidelines and set deadlines for the lower officials to reach agreement on certain disputes. The second strategy is to bring China on board through multilateral settings, such as ASEAN, ARF, ASEAN+3, ADMM Plus, and the East Asia Summit (EAS). In 2010, Vietnam used its ASEAN chairmanship to internationalize the SCS issue by resuming the ASEAN-China Joint Working Group to implement the 2002 DOC. The third strategy is the development of its military capability to deter China from using force. As part of its defensive strategy, Vietnam has offered its Cam Ranh Bay as a repair facility to encourage the presence of international navies in the SCS (Thayer 2011b). A Vietnamese scholar Le Hong Hiep believes that Vietnam's ongoing disputes in the SCS amidst China's emergence as a global power is "arguably the most important variable in the shaping of Vietnam's current perception of China and its contemporary China policy" (Hiep 2013, 340).

Vietnam rejects China's argument that the SCS dispute is bilateral in nature, and therefore, should be addressed bilaterally among the claimant states. For Vietnam, the dispute is bilateral, multilateral and international and cannot be addressed through bilateral discussions alone. The dispute in the Paracels is a bilateral problem between Vietnam and China, but the dispute in the Spratlys is a multilateral problem involving China, Taiwan, Vietnam, the Philippines, Malaysia and Brunei. Issues such as maritime security, freedom and safety of navigation permeates national boundaries. Though China insists that the disputes are bilateral, it is unlikely that it would accept any agreement or settlement among the ASEAN claimant states. What China wants is a bilateral settlement between China and the other claimant states individually (Tuan 2017).

The SCS dispute has shaped Vietnam's policy in three different ways. First, the dispute has revived and reinforced Vietnam's perception of China as an aggressive and expansionist power. Second, it reveals the power asymmetry between the two nations and Vietnam's vulnerabilities in the hands of China. Third, the dispute also gives rise to anti-China nationalism in Vietnam, which prevents the positive role of ideological and cultural affinity as well as the growing economic interdependence between the two nations (Hiep 2013). During my interaction with Hiep, he said that China has occupied some features in the Paracels by driving out the Vietnamese in 1974 and also in the Spratlys, but they have not been able to occupy the entire SCS. And for Vietnam, protecting the sovereignty is the most important issue for the Communist Party, and it will not surrender national sovereignty and territorial integrity under any circumstances. For example, if leaders attempt to abandon, the public will not accept it and there will be domestic violence against the ruler. Vietnam has a very strong nationalist mind coupled with its historical distrust and enmity toward China (Interview on December 22, 2017).

Malaysia's claim and activities

Authors have given differing numbers of Malaysia's claims in the SCS. The Asia Maritime Transparency Initiative gives the number of features occupied by Malaysia in the Spratly Islands as five: Ardasier Reef, Erica Reef, Investigator Shoal, Mariveles Reef and Swallow Reef. All these features are in the southern part of the islands which are closest to the state of Sabah in Malaysia (Asia Maritime Transparency Initiative 2019). However, Captain J. Ashley Roach in his 2014 analytical report published in CNA for a project entitled 'U.S. Policy Options in the South China Sea' puts Malaysia's claims to seven islands or rocks in the Spratly group, two of which are occupied by Vietnam and one by the Philippines, and Malaysia occupies the remaining four where it constructs mini-naval stations with small boat basins on each of the feature. Malaysia also makes claims on two low-tide elevation and three submerged reefs on its continental shelf. Malaysia's claims in the Spratly Islands came with its continental shelf claim in 1979, which it subsequently followed by the publication of a map that was disputed by China, Indonesia, Vietnam and the Philippines (Roach 2014). Unlike these two authors, Prashanth Parameswaran puts Malaysia's claim to 11 maritime features in the Spratly Islands out of which it occupies eight, and the other three are occupied by Vietnam or the Philippines. The claimed 11 features are Ardasier Reef, Dallas Reef, Louisa Reef, Mariveles Reef, Royal Charlotte Reef, Swallow Reef, Erica Reef, Investigator Reef, Commodore Reef, Amboyna Cay and Barque Canada Reef (Parameswaran 2015).

Another scholar puts Malaysia's claims in the SCS to 12 reefs, shoals, and atolls in the Spratlys since 1979 (Lee 2011). Along the line of the Asia Maritime Transparency Initiative, one other scholar writes that Malaysia has a physical presence on five features in the Spratlys by maintaining naval and marine research stations on Terumbu Mantanani (Mariveles Reef), Terumbu Ubi (Ardasier Reef), Terumbu Siput (Erica Reef), Terumbu Peninjau (Investigator Reef) and Pulau Layang-Layang (Swallow Island), which was initially known as Terumbu Layang-Layang or Swallow Reef. With land reclamation, Malaysia has created a 50-acre island on one part of Swallow Reef and has also developed a dive resort. With these constructions, it becomes a popular destination for diving and tourism. Malaysia's occupation of these features has been protested by other claimants. One most notable incident was with Vietnam in the 1980s over Amboyna Cay where Malaysia placed markers in 1978. Vietnam destroyed the markers in 1979 and occupied it. And in order to avoid further escalation of tensions, Malaysia has refrained from any installations in any of its occupied features since the construction of a naval station in Terumbu Siput in 1999 (Noor 2017).

Safeguarding its claims in the SCS is essential for Malaysia's development and security. Malaysia, which is the second-largest oil and natural gas producer in Southeast Asia and the third-largest liquefied natural gas exporter in the world, depends significantly on the oil and gas resources derived from the SCS. The oil and gas sector constitutes about a third of Malaysia's annual revenue, and several of the fields and platforms used to exploit hydrocarbons are situated within the Nine-Dash Line which China claims. Moreover, preventing encroachments from other claimants is essential for preserving Malaysia's sovereignty and territorial integrity since the sea divides peninsular Malaysia from east Malaysia. While China is Malaysia's main rival in the SCS, it is also its largest trading partner and the biggest tourist-generating country outside of ASEAN. Malaysia also does not feel threatened by China as much as Vietnam or the Philippines since its claims are in the southernmost part of the Nine-Dash Line. Malaysia feels that China presents more of an opportunity than a threat, which is why it strengthens its economic relationship with China by ensuring that the SCS issue does not overshadow the bilateral relationship. At the same time, Malaysia believes in a peaceful settlement of the SCS disputes in accordance with international law, such as the UNCLOS. Malaysia also wants to see peace and stability in the region (Parameswaran 2015).

In May 2009, Malaysia and Vietnam made a joint submission to the UN's Commission on the Limits of the Continental Shelf for an extended continental shelf that covers the seabed between Vietnam and the Malaysian states of Sarawa and Sabah, to which China responded furiously. In its protest submitted to the UN secretary-general, China stated that the joint submission violated China's sovereignty rights and jurisdiction (Lee 2011). The Malaysia-China relations became a greater concern in 1995 in the aftermath of the February Mischief Reef incident between China and the Philippines, a fellow ASEAN claimant. Malaysia stood with ASEAN to voice its collective concern over China's aggressive action and reassessed its relations vis-à-vis China on the SCS. In the aftermath of the Mischief incident, the then Malaysian Foreign Minister Abdullah Badawi reportedly said that although China was reluctant to refer the SCS issue to a third party and instead settle among the claimant states, it was necessary to refer to a third party to avoid the escalation of tensions in the region. Following the Mischief Reef incident and Malaysia's concerns, China made an effort to calm the situation and normalize relations with Malaysia. During his visit to Kuala Lumpur in August 1997, Chinese Premier Li Peng proposed a joint development in the disputed Spratlys with ASEAN. After that Malaysia apparently changed its position on China. When tension erupted again between China and the Philippines in November 1998, Malaysia chose to commend the restraint China had shown. Subsequently at the 1999 ASEAN Ministerial meeting in Singapore, Malaysian Foreign Minister Syed Hamid opposed the Philippines' request to discuss the SCS issue at the ARF, and said that the matter should be discussed bilaterally between China and the Philippines. Syed Hamid said it would make the matter more complicated if it is internationalized. Moreover, Malaysia opposed the COC drafted by Vietnam and the Philippines (Liow 2000). As recently as September 2019, the two countries agreed to set up a joint dialogue mechanism to discuss the SCS. After meeting his Malaysian counterpart, Saifuddin Abdullah, in Beijing on September 12, Chinese Foreign Minister Wang Yi said,

> Tensions in the South China Sea have dropped recently. Littoral states and China are committed to appropriately handling the South China Sea issue and jointly safeguarding peace and stability there. . . . To this end, our two sides have agreed to set up a bilateral consultation mechanism for maritime issues. A new platform for dialogue and cooperation.
> (Lo 2019)

Brunei's claim and activities

Brunei is undoubtedly the least vocal in the SCS since its claim is limited compared to the other claimants. It claims the 200 nautical miles of its EEZ under the terms of the UNCLOS, as well as land features within the legally delimited boundaries in the southern portion of the sea, including the Louisa Reef, Owen Shoal and Rifleman Bank. Brunei's claim of its continental shelf uses the same rationale that Malaysia used for its claim in the Spratlys. Malaysia had initially made claim to the Louisa Reef, but apparently dropped it (Roach 2014). Unlike the other claimants, Brunei does not occupy any land features and does not maintain a permanent military base to enforce its claim. But the ground reality suggests that Brunei, which is the silent claimant, has been increasingly reliant on China economically and politically following large investments and improved bilateral relations. In April 2016, Chinese Foreign Minister Wang Yi announced that China had reached a four-point consensus agreement with Brunei, Laos and Cambodia that the dispute in the SCS was not directly concerned with ASEAN and it should rather be resolved between the concerned parties through dialogue and consultations. However, it is not a surprise to see Brunei pursuing an appeasement policy particularly because Brunei needs the economic support of China. Brunei has realized that it cannot rely on its oil and gas reserves for sustained growth. Moreover, the recent decline in global oil prices and the gradual depletion of its oil and gas reserves necessitates Brunei to look for a reliable partner. With Brunei Vision 2035, it plans to restructure its economy with China's assistance (Hart 2018). Kembara has even gone to the point of stating that Brunei receives a lot of Chinese money, which buys their silence (Interview on January 18, 2018). Along similar line, Lean said Brunei-China bilateral ties are very significant to the point that Bandar Seri Begawan is "not willing to rock the boat" (Interview on December 26, 2017). But since Brunei's claim overlaps with the Chinese Nine-Dash Line, one scholar suggests that the likely solution will be a joint exploration with China (Roberts 2011).

Position of Indonesia

Over the years, the role of Indonesia has been limited to being part of the ASEAN team since the country is not one of the active claimants in the SCS. However, from January through June 2016, Indonesia and China engaged in three successive maritime skirmishes, involving warning shots. The June 2016 episode occurred when Indonesian warships challenged a group of Chinese fishing boats operating within Indonesia's 200 mile EEZ off the Natuna Islands. The Indonesian navy fired warning shots to stop the fishing boats and subsequently confiscated a boat and detained a seven-member crew. China protested that the fishing boats were operating in its territory in the SCS and accused Indonesia of violating international laws, including the UNCLOS. Earlier in March and May 2016, Indonesia detained Chinese fishing boats and their crew near the Natuna Islands for a similar reason (Cochrane 2016). Due to frequent conflicts with China over the fishing waters coupled with the Chinese controversial assertion, Indonesian President Joko Widodo traveled to the southern end of the SCS on June 23, 2016, and affirmed his country's sovereignty over waters at the center of a fishing rights dispute between the two nations. Indonesia says that China's Nine-Dash Line that runs through a wide swath of the SCS has no basis under international law (Otto 2016). Another stand-off happened between the two countries in December 2019 which went onto early January 2020 when the Chinese fishing vessels entered Indonesia's EEZ in the Natuna waters prompting Indonesia to summon the Chinese ambassador in Jakarta and deploying eight warships and four fighter jets in the area.

Indonesia is not a direct claimant in the SCS disputes, but China's claims of the Nine-Dash Line overlaps with part of Indonesia's EEZ around the Natuna Islands. Because of the existing ambiguity, Indonesia has since 1994 sought clarification from China whether the Nine-Dash Line includes the Natuna Islands and/or Indonesia's EEZ. In November 2015, China recognized Indonesia's sovereignty over the Natuna Islands but did not address the issue of the EEZ (Cochrane 2016). During my interview with Agusman, he categorically denied Indonesia is a claimant in the SCS because there is no dispute with other claimants with regard to features or titles. For example, China says it does not claim the Natuna Islands. There are also no overlapping claims in maritime rights. Indonesia is also different from Brunei for the fact that Brunei has features within its EEZ which overlaps with China's Nine-Dash Line. That situation does not exist with Indonesia (Interview on January 23, 2018). However, if the contentious dispute between the two countries is not addressed, it has the potential of further escalation. Depending on the role and effectiveness of the arbitral tribunal, one possible scenario is that Indonesia may decide to take its dispute with China to arbitration court. There is also a possibility that Indonesia will find itself inevitably dragged into the issue and become a direct party to the SCS disputes.

Varying levels of claims

Though there are four active claimants within the ASEAN states, apparently there are varying levels of claims and activities among the member states. Undoubtedly, Vietnam and the Philippines are the more vocal claimants. But the question is why some countries are more vocal than the others. Scholars and practitioners, including the Filipinos, have diverse views on the issue. Baviera said Vietnam is in a more difficult position than the Philippines, as it has fought wars with China in the Paracels in 1974 and in the Spratlys in 1988. Therefore, it has a history of conflict that the Philippines does not have with China. Vietnam's membership in ASEAN was a strategic move, partly to balance China out of lack of a viable alternative on the SCS issue. However, Vietnam has been careful about how it proceeds due to its aim of securing economic benefits from China. It also has India as a friend, and others cooperating with Vietnam on oil projects on the continental shelf. The Philippines has been a target of China's assertive action which is demonstrated by the latter's occupation of the Mischief Reef and the Scarborough Shoal since the mid-1990s. If you go by the number of occupied features, Vietnam has the largest stake in the SCS disputes. Malaysia prioritizes its relationship with China especially due to economic considerations. Their claim is less extensive; only a small part of the Nine-Dash Line overlaps with its EEZ. It started its claim in 1979. Brunei has a very small stake, a small corridor. Their problem is primarily with Malaysia and not with China (Interview on December 4, 2017).

Encomienda said the Philippines and Vietnam are the so-called frontline states in the dispute situation, and therefore, face head-on collisions with China. On the other hand, for Brunei and Malaysia, the issue is almost peripheral; there is no big quarrel there for them. Indonesia has no sovereignty issue with China but for a softer concern that China's Nine-Dash Line claim comes close to its Natuna and Anambas Islands; the territorial sea is not affected. The hard issue with the Philippines and Vietnam with regard to sovereignty over islands does not apply to Indonesia. Taiwan holds Itu Aba, the largest island in the Spratlys, but since Taiwan is not a sovereign state, the scope for open involvement is not there. Besides, it is important to mention that the Nine-Dash Line claim was first promulgated by the Kuomintang government in 1947 and not by the PRC. In other words, Beijing is merely a successor government to then Kuomintang China in regard to the Nine-Dash Line claim – the latter entity being the original proponent (Interview on December 1, 2017).

Another Filipino practitioner, Amador, said that before the Duterte administration the Philippines used to be the most vocal, and therefore, it was the primary target of the Chinese government. Vietnam enjoyed a free ride on the Philippines' stature and waited for the tribunal ruling. Vietnam never raised the issue during the ASEAN meetings and instead made efforts not to damage its ties with China. Malaysia prefers not to harm its economic relations with China, but it indirectly supported the Philippines efforts. Brunei recognizes its relatively smaller size and stake in the SCS. Indonesia tries to play the role of an honest broker, but because of China's infringement on the Natuna Islands it has become difficult for Indonesia to remain silent. Taiwan is quiet because its claims are more or less the same as China's due to the fact that it is officially considered a part of China. From a policy perspective, it does not matter because we don't recognize Taiwan as a sovereign nation, and this view is shared by all claimant states in ASEAN (Interview on December 7, 2017).

For Hiep, the Philippines and Vietnam feel the need to be more vocal since they have the biggest claims. The Philippines and China have overlapping claims in Scarborough Shoal and over the Spratlys, including EEZs. Vietnam is of the view that the Spratly features have no EEZs, consistent with the UNCLOS ruling. Now the dispute is over the ownership of those features in the Spratlys which the Philippines controls about 21 percent. The Philippines control seven or eight largest features, larger than what Vietnam is claiming. Most of Vietnam's claims are rocks or smaller features in the Spratlys. They are not like islands. Some reports say Vietnam controls 30–40 percent, but that is not true. Some of them are in the continental shelf. Vietnam claims the entire Paracel Islands. Malaysia and Brunei have limited claims. Brunei's claims are the EEZ and about two rocks in the EEZ which is very insignificant. Malaysia has claims over certain features in the Spratlys but not the entire areas. The problem is more about how ASEAN deals with China and not necessarily among ASEAN member states. Previously, there was an argument that Vietnam's claims overlap with the EEZs of other claimant states. After the 2016 UNCLOS ruling, which said none of the features is an island, there is no question of an EEZ issue here. The EEZ issue becomes irrelevant. But Vietnam has not released an official statement on the contents of the UNCLOS ruling to make its claim ambiguous, like the Chinese Nine-Dash Line claim (Interview on December 22, 2017).

ASEAN position and its challenges

ASEAN, as an organization, became involved in the SCS disputes in July 1992 when China and Vietnam embroiled themselves in exploration activities. Though Vietnam was not yet a member, ASEAN issued a statement urging restraint in the area. Both China and Vietnam did not pay attention to the call and instead took control of the unoccupied islets and reefs in the Spratly archipelago near Brunei, Malaysia and the Philippines. In late 1994, ASEAN issued a second statement urging the concerned parties to restrain from taking actions that could destabilize the situation when China occupied the Mischief Reef claimed by the Philippines. The incident was a turning point in which the Philippines lobbied its fellow ASEAN members to adopt a COC that will prevent China from encroaching. It took ASEAN nearly five years to agree on the draft by the time China had also drawn up its own draft (Thayer 2013).

Over the years, ASEAN has taken certain steps to address problems surrounding the SCS, despite its own internal differences. At the 24th ASEAN Summit in May 2014, foreign ministers of the regional bloc released a statement expressing their serious concerns over the increased tension in the SCS. The statement urged all concerned parties to exercise restraint from taking actions that could undermine peace and stability and to resolve all disputes by peaceful means through the universally recognized principles of international law, including UNCLOS. The leaders reaffirmed the importance of maintaining peace and stability, maritime security, freedom of navigation and overflight above the SCS, the ASEAN six-point principles on the SCS and the joint statement of the 15th ASEAN-China Summit on the 10th anniversary of the DOC, a statement jointly released in 2002 by ASEAN and China. The statement also called on all concerned parties to fully and effectively implement the DOC to create an environment of mutual trust and confidence (ASEAN 2014).

The SCS disputes involve four of the ten ASEAN members – Brunei, Malaysia, the Philippines, and Vietnam. Since the formation of ASEAN in 1967, one of its objectives has been to preserve the sovereignty of member states, to prevent the Southeast Asian region from interference by outside powers and to assert itself in regional security affairs. However, lingering SCS disputes have become an obstacle to achieving these objectives. ASEAN's problem is not only with China but also within its own members for their inability to come up with a unified SCS policy while recognizing that the sovereignty disputes will have to be resolved by the claimants. ASEAN also has a difficulty of asserting its centrality in regional security affairs. Traditionally, the two fundamental principles of ASEAN since its formation have been non-interference in the internal affairs of member states and reaching an agreement by consensus. In recent years, ASEAN has taken several initiatives to integrate member countries, including developing a single market that would ensure the free flow of goods, services, investment and skilled labor, and the free flow of capital. Nonetheless, the region is far from being homogeneous and encompassing with different political institutions, diverse languages and cultures. Because of the geostrategic location and its emerging economies, the region has become of greater interest to its neighboring countries as well as the Western democracies.

The central problem is the claim of overlapping areas by different countries involving Brunei, China, Vietnam, the Philippines, Taiwan and Malaysia. One of the fundamental principles of ASEAN has been to resolve disputes by peaceful means and to reach agreements by consensus. But over the years, the position of ASEAN on the SCS disputes has been weak. At times, the organization has been unable to formulate a consensus policy. This is partly due to the fact that not all ten ASEAN members are claimants to the SCS. Another reason is that ASEAN members have overlapping claims among themselves. Moreover, bilateral relations between China and some smaller ASEAN members, such as Laos and Cambodia, are also a factor. Because of its economic and military powers, China has been able to win over or coopt some ASEAN members. One example of ASEAN's inability to reach a consensus agreement was on June 15, 2016, when it retracted a statement expressing deep concerns over the tensions in the SCS. The statement, released by the Malaysian foreign ministry, did not name China but warned the rising tensions in the sea where Beijing has been building artificial islands and also increases its military presence. The statement was released after a meeting of foreign ministers from ASEAN and China in Kunming, China. Within hours of releasing the statement, the Malaysian foreign ministry recalled it on the ground that it needed "urgent amendments" without specifying the details. The foreign ministry spokeswoman later said that ASEAN members will issue individual statements. The initial statement reiterated ASEAN's existing concerns over the artificial islands as well as the militarization of the region and also countered China's position that the disputes should be settled between the parties concerned and not between ASEAN and China. The ASEAN-China meeting took place before the tribunal ruling at The Hague on a case petitioned by the Philippines contesting Beijing's claim in the SCS (Latiff 2016). Subsequently, on July 15, 2016, Cambodian Prime Minister Hun Sen announced that China will give Cambodia almost $600 million in aid to support election infrastructure, education and health projects. Again, on July 25, 2016, ASEAN was forced to avoid criticizing China on the SCS disputes because of objection from Cambodia (British Broadcasting Corporation 2016).

China is well aware that a united voice of all ASEAN members would have greater leverage. ASEAN's inability to build a united front on the SCS disputes is a major challenge for the regional bloc. There is no single country in ASEAN party to the SCS disputes that is capable of challenging China individually. This is an important reason why some within ASEAN have welcomed the role of the US as a power balancer. While China insists on talks between the parties concerned, the claimants in ASEAN want to pursue multilaterally or through arbitration. The existence of two diametrically opposing approaches is a major challenge to reach a mutually acceptable solution on the SCS disputes. Since China has openly refused to acknowledge or accept the tribunal ruling, despite support from several countries, and because of the lack of enforcement power, this mechanism is likely to be inconclusive. However, the international community's reaction in the aftermath of the arbitration is bound to put pressure on China. The ruling can also provide a basis or justification for future coalition actions.

Conclusion

This chapter examines the claims and activities of other claimant states (other than China) – Taiwan, the Philippines, Vietnam, Malaysia, and Brunei – as well as the efforts and challenges of ASEAN as a collective body. Taiwan suffers an identity crisis because of the adherence to one-China policy by all other claimant states. The Philippines and Vietnam have been visibly more vocal on their claims but they are unable to do much in the face of the rising China. Malaysia and Brunei have largely been silent because of their individual political and economic ties with China. ASEAN has collectively engaged through the DOC and COC but has been unable to achieve an amicable agreement, either due to the competing claims among themselves or China's insistence on a bilateral solution. The role of Indonesia has been limited to being part of the ASEAN team since the country is not one of the active claimants. However, from January through June 2016, Indonesia and China engaged in three successive maritime skirmishes involving warning shots. Another tension erupted in December 2019 which went onto early January 2020. If the contentious dispute between the two countries is not addressed, it has the potential of further escalation. There is also a possibility that Indonesia will find itself inevitably dragged into the issue and becoming a direct party to the SCS disputes.

4 The July 2016 arbitral tribunal award

The arbitral tribunal gave its ruling on the SCS dispute on a case filed by the Philippines at the PCA at The Hague in July 2016, and some have argued that the verdict has wider implications beyond China and the Philippines (Singh 2016). Before discussing the arbitration proceedings, it is essential to understand some background information and provisions of the Law of the Sea Convention or the Law of the Sea treaty, popularly known as UNCLOS, which is the international agreement that resulted from the third UN Conference on the Law of the Sea that took place between 1973 and 1982. The case between the Philippines and China was decided by the arbitral tribunal constituted under Annex VII of the UNCLOS.

The UNCLOS

The UNCLOS establishes a legal framework for managing disputes in the oceans and provides a legal mechanism to facilitate communication between states through a peaceful, equitable and efficient use of the oceans. Under the UNCLOS, coastal states are entitled to certain maritime zones, including a territorial sea up to 12 nautical miles from its land territory where they can exercise complete sovereignty over the water, seabed, and subsoil. A coastal or littoral state may also exercise sovereign rights over a continental shelf of up to 200 nautical miles from its land territory for the purpose of exploration and exploitation of the natural resources in the seabed and subsoil of the submarine areas. A coastal state is also entitled to an EEZ of 200 nautical miles from its land territory with the sovereign rights for exploring and exploiting the living and non-living resources. Within this area, the state has the jurisdictional rights to establish and use for putting up structures, such as artificial islands and/or other installations. Offshore features are also titled maritime zones but it depends on how such features are classified, such as a rock, low tide elevation, or artificial island. An island, which is a naturally formed area of land that remains above water at high tide, is entitled to the same maritime zones, such as 12 nautical miles of territorial sea, and 200 nautical miles of EEZ and continental shelf. Rocks are a sub-category of islands so long as they remain above water at high tide.

But since they cannot sustain human habitation or economic life of their own, rocks are entitled to only 12 nautical miles of territorial sea. A low tide elevation, a naturally formed area of land that remains above water at low tide but is submerged at high tide, may be used as a baseline for measuring a coastal state's territorial sea. But if the low tide elevation exists beyond the 12 nautical miles of the coastal state, it does not have a territorial sea of its own. An artificial island is also not entitled to any maritime zones with the exception of a 500-meter safety zone. The UNCLOS provides definitions for classifying offshore features but does not contain provisions to decide competing sovereignty claims by states (Kingdon 2015).

Though UNCLOS cannot help resolve competing claims over sovereignty matters, it has a provision for settling disputes between parties over the interpretation or application of its provisions. When two states are involved in a dispute over the interpretation or application of the provisions, they are subject to a compulsory binding dispute settlement. First, states are obligated to find a peaceful solution through the process outlined in Section 1 of Part XV. Under Article 282, if the disputing parties have agreed through a general, regional or bilateral agreement for a binding decision, that procedure will be utilized in lieu of the UNCLOS procedure. If no settlement is reached between the two parties under Section 1 of Part XV, either of the party may submit the case to a court or arbitration under Section 2 of Part XV. After signing and ratifying the UNCLOS, a state, under Article 287, is free to choose one or more of the four possible channels for settling disputes with regard to the interpretation or application: a state may elect to adjudicate before ITLOS; adjudicate before ICJ; arbitrate before an Annex VII tribunal; or arbitrate before a special tribunal under Annex VIII. Only if both parties agree to the same procedure for settlement will the dispute be submitted to that procedure. If the parties do not agree on the same procedure or any one of the four procedures, the dispute can be submitted to Annex VII arbitration, and any decision under such arbitration is final and binding on all parties to the dispute. Also, under Article 287 of the UNCLOS, a state may agree to settle the dispute through ITLOS or ICJ. While both tribunals have extensive jurisdiction, the claims brought before ITLOS are limited in number and scope. But ITLOS is granted compulsory jurisdiction to hear urgent issues or cases for provisional measures, although an arbitral tribunal for final determination has not been formed for it yet. On the other hand, ICJ acts as the adjudicatory arm of the UN for dispute settlement under UNCLOS (Kingdon 2015).

The Annex VII arbitral tribunals under Article 287 have increasingly become an important venue for dispute settlement. The Annex VII tribunal consists of five members: each party to the proceeding may appoint one member each and the remaining three members are appointed by the agreement of both parties. If the parties cannot reach an agreement on the three members, the president of ITLOS will appoint them. If one of the parties to the dispute fails to appear before the tribunal, the other may request for the proceeding to continue and deliver the award. The arbitral tribunal's award is final and may not be appealed (Kingdon 2015). With regard to historical rights claims, though they are established by international law, the question remains whether the impending imposition of UNCLOS and the resultant activation of the EEZ and continental shelf regimes actually nullifies states' title to such rights. The question pertains to the legal conflicts between the EEZ or continental shelf regimes and states' historical rights claims. If there is no conflict, Article 311(2) of the UNCLOS ensures that the historical rights regime remains intact. But if there is a conflict, the EEZ and continental shelf systems prevail over states' continental shelf claims (Korkut and Kang 2017).

Some events before arbitration

On January 22, 2013, the Philippines under Benigno Aquino III instituted arbitral proceeding against China under Article 287 and Annex VII of the UNCLOS with respect to maritime jurisdictional disputes between the Philippines and China in the Spratly Islands. The move was significant in the sense that it was the first international litigation initiated by a claimant state on the SCS. It was considered a bold move by the Philippines that could have served as a game changer in the whole SCS disputes. The Philippines took a decision to approach the tribunal after a series of provocative and aggressive activities from China, including a tense confrontation between the two countries in April 2012 over the Scarborough Shoal. This was considered the gravest situation between the two littoral states since the Mischief Reef incident in 1994 (Bautista 2014). In response to the Philippines move, China on February 19, 2013, declared that it would neither accept nor participate in the arbitration proceedings (Zhang 2017).

China maintained that its 2006 declaration under Article 298 of the United Nations Division for Ocean Affairs and the Law of the Sea (UNDOALS) covered the dispute brought forth by the Philippines. On December 7, 2014, China published a paper outlining its position on the issue. But on October 29, 2015, the arbitral tribunal ruled that it has jurisdiction over the case and took up seven of the 15 submissions made by the Philippines.

The August 25, 2006, declaration under Article 298 of UNDOALS (made after its ratification on June 7, 1996) states that:

1 In accordance with the provisions of the United Nations Convention on the Law of the Sea, the People's Republic of China shall enjoy sovereign rights and jurisdiction over an exclusive economic zone (EEZ) of 200 nautical miles and the continental shelf.
2 The People's Republic of China will effect, through consultations, the delimitation of the boundary of the maritime jurisdiction with the States with coasts opposite or adjacent to China respectively on the basis of international law and in accordance with the principle of equitability.

3 The People's Republic of China reaffirms its sovereignty over all its archipelagos and islands as listed in article 2 of the Law of the People's Republic of China on the territorial sea and the contiguous zone, which was promulgated on 25 February 1992.

4 The People's Republic of China reaffirms that the provisions of the United Nations Convention on the Law of the Sea concerning innocent passage through the territorial sea shall not prejudice the right of a coastal State to request, in accordance with its laws and regulations, a foreign State to obtain advance approval from or give prior notification to the coastal State for the passage of its warships through the territorial sea of the coastal State.

(Oceans & Law of the Sea, United Nations 2013)

The latest round of tensions between the Philippines and China intensified after the latter gained de facto control of the Scarborough Shoal in 2012. In recent years, attention has shifted to China's construction and installation of military-capable infrastructures in the Spratly Islands. The pace and scale of China's island-building works have dwarfed the presence of other claimants and is beginning to take on a more overtly strategic character, which includes the construction of runways and port facilities. Amid the ongoing tensions, the Chinese foreign ministry on May 20, 2016, claimed that more than 40 countries of the world have supported its position on a case filed at the PCA by the Philippines, contesting the legality of China's claim of the Nine-Dash Line. China refused to recognize the case and claimed that all disputes in the SCS should be resolved among the concerned parties. Beijing's position is that any neutral country would support its position on the issue. The Chinese Foreign Ministry spokeswoman, Hua Chunying, said "More and more countries are expressing themselves and showing their support for China on the South China Sea issue" (Rajagopalan 2016). The Chinese Nine-Dash Line stretches deep into the maritime heart of Southeast Asia, covering hundreds of disputed islands and reefs, rich fishing grounds and oil and gas deposits through which trillions of dollars in shipborne trade passes every year.

In a letter to the *New York Times* on May 31, 2016, press counselor and spokesman for the Chinese embassy in Washington, DC, Zhu Haiquan, defended China's refusal to recognize or participate in the proceedings of the PCA. He reiterated China's historical claim of sovereignty over the SCS and that the lingering disputes should be settled through negotiation between the concerned states. The letter further said:

> China is exercising its legitimate rights by upholding the sovereignty of our islands in the South China Sea. China's sovereignty over the Nansha Islands and Xisha Islands was restored after World War II, in accordance with the Cairo Declaration and the Potsdam Proclamation. But in the 1970s, certain countries started to illegally occupy some islands

> and reefs of the Nansha Islands. Negotiation between states directly concerned is the only way to resolve the disputes. China has already signed border treaties through peaceful negotiations with 12 out of 14 land neighbors. The same practice should be adopted in the South China Sea. While pursuing diplomatic resolution, China is exercising restraint. The construction activities on the islands and reefs are all for peaceful purposes and do not affect in any way freedom of navigation and overflight. By not accepting or participating in the arbitration unilaterally initiated by the Philippines, China is acting in accordance with international law.
>
> (Haiquan 2016)

Apart from its refusal to recognize the Philippines' petition at the PCA, China is wary of any interference from other countries. Over the years, Beijing has urged or warned other nations from meddling in the SCS disputes. One such instance was in May 2016, when Beijing warned the leaders of the Group of Seven nations (commonly known as G7) not to engage in actions that could exacerbate tensions. However, the heads of states from Britain, Canada, France, Germany, Italy, Japan and the US said it was necessary to send a strong message regarding the maritime disputes. Earlier, during the gathering of G7 foreign ministers in April 2016, the leaders issued a joint statement concerning maritime security expressing a strong opposition to coercive and provocative actions that could change the status quo. Tensions have been high particularly between China and the Philippines since June 2012, when Beijing seized control of the Scarborough Shoal following a three-month-long confrontation after a Philippine naval vessel tried to arrest the Chinese fishermen who were illegally catching giant clams (Pinghui 2016).

Award of Permanent Court of Arbitration

The tribunal was formed on June 21, 2013, under Annex VII of the UNCLOS to adjudicate on a case filed by the Philippines. The tribunal was composed of Judge Thomas A. Mensah of Ghana, Judge Jean-Pierre Cot of France, Judge Stanislaw Pawlak of Poland, Professor Alfred H.A. Soons of the Netherlands, and Judge Rüdiger Wolfrum of Germany. Judge Thomas A. Mensah served as president of the tribunal. The PCA acted as the registry in the proceedings (PCA Press Release 2016). The case between the Philippines and China, decided by the arbitral tribunal under Annex VII, was the first decision by an international tribunal to elaborate on Article 121(3) of the UNCLOS (Korkut and Kang 2017). On June 30, 2016, days before the arbitral tribunal gave its ruling, the Chinese Foreign Ministry spokesman, Hong Lei, said:

> I again stress that the arbitration court has no jurisdiction in the case and on the relevant matter, and should not hold hearings or make a

> ruling. . . . The Philippines' unilateral lodging of the South China Sea arbitration case is contrary to international law. . . . On the issue of territory and disputes over maritime delineation, China does not accept any dispute resolution from a third party and does not accept any dispute resolution forced on China.

The Chinese government said the Philippines' action flouted international law and could only worsen the SCS disputes, which it claims about 90 percent of it (Blanchard and Deutsch 2016).

After three years of deliberation, the tribunal gave its ruling on the dispute between China and the Philippines on July 12, 2016, in favor of the latter. The tribunal concluded that there was no legal basis for China to claim historic rights to resources within the sea areas falling within the Nine-Dash Line and that the Chinese vessels had unlawfully created a serious risk of collision by physically obstructing the Philippines' vessels. In a statement, the tribunal said:

> Having found that certain areas are within the exclusive economic zone of the Philippines, the tribunal found that China had violated the Philippines' sovereign rights in its EEZ by (a) interfering with Philippines fishing and petroleum exploration, (b) constructing artificial islands and (c) failing to prevent Chinese fishermen from fishing in the zone.
>
> (Santos 2016)

The tribunal ruled that none of the disputed islands, including Itu Aba (Taiping Island), the largest naturally formed feature which is occupied by Taiwan, is entitled to an EEZ and continental shelf of their own. This means that all islands in the Spratlys, as well as the Scarborough Shoal, are at most rocks and are entitled to only a 12-nautical mile of territorial sea. The arbitration means that there are no overlapping EEZ claims between China and the other Southeast Asian claimants. Several of the reefs occupied by China are low-tide elevations rather than islands, and therefore, they cannot be subject to sovereignty claims unless they are within 12 nautical miles of an island. Moreover, they are not entitled to any maritime zones. The tribunal also ruled that both the Mischief Reef and the Second Thomas Shoal are low-tide elevations within the EEZ of the Philippines. However, with its land reclamation and construction work, China has made the Mischief Reef the largest island in the SCS at no less than 5.6 kilometers in size. The arbitration supported 14 out of 15 claims made by the Philippines, which significantly has reduced the claims of China in the Spratlys and the Scarborough Shoal (Zhang 2017).

Though China maintained that the tribunal had no jurisdiction over its SCS dispute with the Philippines, the tribunal argued that it had the jurisdiction to consider the historical rights and the source of maritime entitlements. The tribunal concluded that China's claim of historical rights to resources in the waters of the SCS violates the EEZ of other littoral states. The tribunal also noted that though Chinese navigators and fishermen and those of other states historically made use of the islands, there was no evidence to claim that China had exclusive control over the waters or the resources. Therefore, there was no legal basis for China to make claim of historical rights within the Nine-Dash Line. While China had extensive land reclamation and physical construction in the reefs China has control of, the tribunal said classification of features under UNCLOS is based on its original condition and historical materials. Under the UNCLOS, islands are entitled to 200 nautical miles of EEZ and continental shelf. But rocks which cannot sustain human habitation or economic life of their own cannot be entitled to both EEZ and continental shelf. The features what China has occupied with its military personnel are receiving support from outside. The tribunal noted that the Spratly Islands were historically used by small groups of fishermen, including those from Japan. The tribunal concluded that none of the Spratly Islands is capable of generating extended maritime zones. Since none of the features claimed by China is capable of generating an EEZ, the tribunal concluded that certain sea areas are within the EEZ of the Philippines. What the tribunal did not address was the issue of sovereignty over land territory, nor did it delimit the boundary between the claimant states (PCA Press Release 2016).

Though the July 2016 arbitration was on a case filed by the Philippines, it was not the only country which had brought the SCS dispute to the PCA. In fact, in 2014, Vietnam had also submitted its case to the PCA. Though China did not file a case, it published a position paper, while the US also issued its position. In its petition, Vietnam asked the PCA to declare its jurisdiction over the SCS and recognize its rights and interests in the Spratly and Paracel Islands, as well as its EEZ and continental shelf, and declare that China's Nine-Dash Line has no legal basis. Moreover, on December 11, 2014, the Vietnamese Foreign Ministry Spokesman Le Hai Binh reiterated his country's claim in the SCS by making the following remarks to the press:

> Once again, Viet Nam reiterates that Viet Nam has full historical evidence and legal foundation to reaffirm its sovereignty over the Hoang Sa [Paracel Islands] and Truong Sa [Spratly Islands] archipelagoes, as well as other legal rights and interests of Viet Nam in the East Sea [Biển Đông]. It is Vietnam's consistent position to fully reject China's claim over the Hoang Sa and Truong Sa archipelagoes and the adjacent waters, as well as China's claiming of "historic rights" to the waters, sea-bed and subsoil within the "dotted line" unilaterally stated by China.
>
> (Calvo 2015, 2)

China's reaction

China had maintained that it did not recognize the tribunal and argued that Manila's case was an issue of territorial sovereignty which the tribunal had no jurisdiction. After the tribunal's ruling, China vowed to protect its sovereignty over the SCS and claimed that it has the right to set up an air defense zone. Beijing accused the PCA at The Hague of being a "puppet" of external forces. China attempted to defend its position of not acknowledging or participating in the proceedings, which one writer described it as an "innately flawed" strategy. Invoking Article 298 of the UNCLOS, China cited its voluntary opt-out of compulsory arbitration. Beijing also unsuccessfully petitioned for the dismissal of the Philippines' case by invoking the DOC in the SCS (Singh 2017, 3).

President Xi Jinping said China's "territorial sovereignty and marine rights" in the SCS would not be affected by the arbitral ruling. The Chinese state media, Xinhua, described the verdict as an "ill-founded" ruling and it was "naturally null and void." The Communist Party mouthpiece newspaper, the *People's Daily*, carried in its editorial that the tribunal had ignored "basic truths" and "trampled" on international laws and norms. The paper further added that "The Chinese government and the Chinese people firmly oppose [the ruling] and will neither acknowledge it nor accept it" (Phillips, Holmes and Bowcott 2016). In a strong response statement to the tribunal's ruling, China said two new airports in the Spratlys – Mischief Reef and Subi Reef – both received test flights from civilian aircraft on July 13, 2016. China has built massive structures including radar systems and airstrips in the disputed area. One major concern of China in the aftermath of the court's ruling was the upsurge of pressures, or even threats, from the international community. A day after the arbitral ruling, Vice Foreign Minister Liu Zhenmin said,

> We hope that other countries don't use this opportunity to threaten China, and hope that other countries can work hard with China, meet us halfway, and maintain the South China Sea's peace and stability and not turn the South China Sea into a source of war.
>
> (Blanchard and Petty 2016)

While China defended its position and action in the SCS, the tribunal concluded that certain areas of the Chinese claim are within the EEZ of the Philippines, and therefore, China has violated the Philippines sovereign rights within its EEZ in three ways: by interfering with Philippine fishing and petroleum exploration; by constructing artificial islands; and by failing to prevent Chinese fishermen from fishing in the zone. The tribunal concluded that fishermen from the Philippines have the traditional fishing rights in the Scarborough Shoal and that China had interfered in this by restricting their access. The arbitration also concluded that Chinese law enforcement vessels had unlawfully created a serious risk of collision when they physically obstructed Philippine vessels in the Scarborough Shoal. China's recent large-scale land reclamation and construction of artificial islands in seven features over the Spratly Islands caused serious harm to the coral reef environment and also violated its obligation to protect and preserve the ecosystems of the habitat of a depleted, threatened and endangered species. The Chinese authorities have not stopped its fishermen from engaging in activities, such as harvesting sea turtles, coral and giant clams in the SCS. The tribunal said it lacked a jurisdiction to rule over the escalated tension between the Philippine marines and Chinese naval and law enforcement vessels at Second Thomas Shoal since the dispute involved military activities, and therefore, excluded it from compulsory settlement. However, the tribunal said China's recent large-scale land reclamation and construction of artificial islands were incompatible with the obligations of a state when the dispute proceedings were underway (PCA Press Release 2016). The underlying issue was that though China refused to accept the arbitration on the ground that it was a unilateral action taken by the Philippines, Article 9 of Annex VII of the UNCLOS states:

> If one of the parties to the dispute does not appear before the arbitral tribunal or fails to defend its case, the other party may request the tribunal to continue the proceedings and to make its award. Absence of a party or failure of a party to defend its case shall not constitute a bar to the proceedings.
>
> (United Nations Convention on the Law of the Sea)

The Philippines' response

Filipinos across the globe welcomed the arbitral ruling, which was considered to be in their favor. The Philippines Foreign Affairs Secretary Perfecto Yasay said, "The Philippines strongly affirms its respect for this milestone decision as an important contribution to ongoing efforts in addressing disputes in the South China Sea." At the same time, he called for "restraint and sobriety," which disappointed many Filipinos, some of whom even accused him of trying to please China. But former President Benigno Aquino III, who initiated the case against China in 2013, urged the international community to use the ruling to resolve maritime disputes and said,

> Instead of viewing this decision as a victory of one party over another, the best way to look at this judgment is that it is a victory for all. I say this because the clarity rendered now establishes better conditions that enable countries to engage each other, bearing in mind their duties and rights within a context that espouses equality and amity.

Senate President Franklin Drilon said the ruling would finally allow "ASEAN and China (to) move forward (and) finalize the Code of Conduct to ensure peace and stability in the South China Sea." Davao Congressman Pantaleon Alvarez said, "We should urge China as part of the community of nations to respect the decision of the arbitral court and adhere to the peaceful settlement of territorial disputes in accordance with international law." Former Justice Secretary and now Senator Leila De Lima, advising the government of President Rodrigo Duterte, said,

> It is hoped that the present Administration will be properly guided in its future actions, especially in its declared bias for bilateral talks which has only proven to be always one-sided in favor of the world power at the other end of the table.

De Lima added that there is now a legal foundation to challenge China's "expansionist moves." Senior Associate Justice Antonio Carpio, who has done several studies on the SCS issue said,

> The ruling also re-affirms UNCLOS as the Constitution for the oceans of our planet, a treaty ratified by 167 States, including China and the Philippines. . . . The ruling applies the fundamental law of the sea principle that "land dominates the sea," that is, any claim to maritime zones must emanate from land and can extend only to the limits prescribed under UNCLOS.
>
> (Palatino 2016)

Shift of strategy under President Rodrigo Duterte?

Banlaoi, a Filipino scholar who teaches at the Department of International Studies of Miriam College and who is also Vice President of the Philippine Association for Chinese Studies, believed that the Duterte administration has changed its strategy in Philippines-China relations. In his commentary *Duterte Presidency: Shift in Philippine-China Relations*, Banlaoi analyzed that contrary to the previous administration, the Duterte government has expressed its serious interest to resume dialogue with China. If this comes to pass, it promises to be a game changer in Philippines-China relations. He added that though the Filipino public continues to disapprove of the Chinese assertiveness in the SCS through island building, construction development and facility improvement in areas which are considered by the Philippines as an integral part of its EEZ, the electoral victory of Duterte seems to suggest that the Filipinos approve his approach on the SCS, that is, to hold bilateral discussions with China and to peacefully manage the disputes, which his predecessor largely ignored. Banlaoi said while Duterte may likely set aside the tribunal award in light of his efforts to reestablish the damaged political ties between the two countries, however, it is unlikely that his administration will withdraw from the arbitration process because of domestic and international considerations. Domestically, the arbitration case has the approval of not only the Filipino public but also key national leaders including past presidents, the senate president, the speaker of the house, justices of the supreme court and concerned department secretaries.

Internationally, the arbitration has the support of the Philippines' security ally the US, and other strategic partners, such as Australia, Japan, South Korea, as well as key members of the European Union (EU) (Banlaoi 2016).

To understand Duterte's government foreign policy and his strategic recalibration toward China, Richard Javad Heydarian, a Filipino commentator and author, discussed in his work *Duterte's Geopolitical Game-Play* that it is important to analyze five key elements. The first is that Duterte's political success is built on an "anti-establishment" brand of populism, which is a rejection of Philippine political elites and their policies. The second is the "authoritarianization" of Philippine political system by concentrating the country's power in his hands. The third element is the lack of a clear commitment from the US in the SCS. The fourth element is that while the Obama administration refused to clarify whether it would come to defend the Philippines in the event of a conflict with China in the SCS, China offered both maritime and economic concessions in exchange for the Philippines setting aside the arbitration issue, and possibly downgrading its ties with the US. President Duterte considered a joint development with China over the Scarborough Shoal, as well as billions of dollars in infrastructural investments. The fifth element is Duterte's "personalization" of foreign policy, not only by concentrating the country's power in his hands but also by injecting his personal emotion in the policy making process. Duterte's tirade against Obama and the US has largely been triggered by the fact that the latter criticized Duterte's campaign against drugs in his first few months in office. On the other hand, China was supportive of Duterte's policy on drugs and offered to help in terms of logistics, equipment, criminal investigation and establishment of rehabilitation centers (Heydarian 2017).

Now the larger question is why did the Philippines decide to pursue the case through arbitration (PCA) when it was evident that China would not accept or cooperate with it? And given the arbitral ruling in favor of the Philippines, why did other claimants not pursue the same route? Here, I will present various viewpoints from people who are directly affected by the ruling or the analyses of experts whom I personally sat down with.

First, on the question of why did the Philippines decide to pursue the case through arbitration when it was evident that China would not accept or cooperate with it, Baviera, a Filipino scholar and someone who has done extensive research and writings on the SCS, said the Philippines had exhausted all possible means on the issue, whether bilateral or ASEAN-led multilateral discussions. The COC did not go forward and neither did the DOC. There were very limited options left. The Philippines followed its political culture of relying on international law and its institutions. Moreover, through the years, the US position on the issue remained stagnant and limited only to freedom of navigation, which was narrow, and therefore, did not converge with the Philippines interests (Interview on December 4, 2017). Along similar line, Naval said it was due to a lack of available alternatives through the diplomatic channel. Left with no other options, it was necessary for the Philippines to pursue the case through arbitration. Since the Philippines military is relatively inferior to China, it was necessary for the Philippines to approach other means which do not rely on the military. The Aquino government said it was a futile exercise to talk to China because Beijing continued to expand its presence and activities in the SCS. Under the Duterte government, there is not much reaction from the local people, especially from the lower-income group as the matter is too complicated for the common people to grapple with. When it comes to international law, Duterte essentially says now is not the time to invoke it (Interview on December 6, 2017).

Batongbacal, another Filipino scholar, said there are three reasons as to why the Philippines pursued the arbitration route. First, at the time (2012–2013), the Philippines under President Aquino saw no options other than arbitration, and it believed that negotiations would not help. China already took control of the Scarborough Shoal, and there was no other way for the Philippines to push back China on this issue. Second, it is also due to the Philippines' culture. The Filipinos tend to respond to or seek an end to conflicts usually by involving or seeking the intervention of third parties. This happens in personal and domestic issues as well. They perceive resolution by neutral and impartial third parties to be the most acceptable and fair means to settlement of disputes. Third, it was also due to the breakdown of relations between China and the Philippines. The two countries were not talking to each other. China wanted the arbitration case be dropped, whereas the Philippines insisted that the case be resolved first before further talks begin (Interview on November 30, 2017).

Amador was of the view that if the Philippines invoked tribunals such as the ICJ or others, then China could have opted out. Under the articles of the UNCLOS, it was a legal strategy to make sure that the ruling was concluded even if China did not participate. The president of ITLOS has the authority over the arbitral tribunal to decide the case. It was a strategic point in the diplomatic angle that China disregarded the proceedings and the ruling. The tribunal took extra pains and efforts to ensure that China's concerns were also taken into consideration, not just the interests of the Philippines. The tribunal said it had jurisdiction on the issue and would give its ruling even if China did not participate. Therefore, whether China recognizes it or not, the arbitration is a decision against China forever. Thus, the ruling is still relevant, that is, the tribunal decision officially says that China does not have the legal basis to its claims in the SCS. Even if China does not recognize the ruling, the Philippines does, and as a result, it becomes part of the Philippines law (Interview on December 7, 2017).

But for Papa, filing the case at the PCA by the Aquino administration was a little bit of a hardline approach. The government was trying to get some leverage on China, with the knowledge that it may not be enforceable, as China may not comply. The Duterte government changed the policy and adopted a friendlier approach toward China. Duterte said he would use the arbitral ruling at another opportune time. The future becomes foggy from here on with an immediate need for bilateral talks, the first of its kind (Interview on December 7, 2017). And for Bata, the bargaining power for a small nation like the Philippines against a giant power like China is through international law (Interview on November 29, 2017).

But different from my other interviewees, Encomienda said earlier in the conflict situation, the Philippines did not see it in the national interest to pursue the case through arbitration; its early direction was to address the situation as a non-traditional regional maritime security concern – in other words, through regional ocean governance cooperation. Arbitration was an American strategy that was suggested during the San Francisco Conference on International Organization in 1945. There was a US internal memo that favored arbitration. Fast-forward to the UNCLOS era and an intensifying regional disputes situation, and the Philippines took into consideration UNCLOS Annex VII on arbitration. This was not pursued as it was decided that a unilateral compulsory arbitration carries a rather "hostile" tone and may not be constructive and conducive toward good relations with the "Colossus of the North," China. It was an untested and novel (unilateral and compulsory) third-party recourse that calls for a cautious approach (Interview on December 1, 2017).

And given the arbitral ruling in favor of the Philippines, why other claimants did not pursue the same route is another question explored in this chapter. The author's interactions with experts and people who are involved on the issue shed light on the different aspects. Djalal believed that it was because the other countries think that the other party would not agree. In the SCS's case, there is no agreement among the claimant states to go to the court. In fact, ASEAN countries have their internal quarrel. For example, the Philippines and Malaysia have territorial and boundary disputes which they need to settle first. They probably think that going to the court will not solve the problem because China will not agree to it. The court's decision provides some clarity but does not solve the problem. The Philippines wanted to or was trying to embarrass China, but fortunately or unfortunately, China does not seem to be embarrassed (Interview on January 19, 2018).

Tavares said one of the reasons is that the Philippines already represented the views of other claimants. What's the point of repeating the same process unless their case will be different? Say, for example, going to the international court to decide on the delimitation of maritime border disputes. In other words, it will be a repetitive exercise for others. A lot of resources would be wasted for a possible outcome that is pretty much the same (Interview on January 20, 2018). Along a similar line, Hikmahanto said other claimants are not pursuing because the Philippines has already done it and others are behind the Philippines. The issue is about the validity of the historical claims made by China. It was also clear that China would not take part in any similar arbitration process. It would have been a redundant exercise for other claimants to pursue the same route. The question is also that whether countries are willing to go head-to-head with China (Interview on January 18, 2018). Staff members of the Centre for Political Studies, Indonesian Institute of Science, were of the view that it was important for the Philippines to prove that China's claims on historical rights and indisputable sovereignty issues have no legal basis. Though the UNCLOS has no authority over sovereignty issues, it was important as a precedent. Now China has agreed to discuss the COC, which can be said to be indirectly related to the arbitral ruling. Also, the Philippines wanted to set a precedent on the issue for other claimant states so that they can base their strategy on this ruling (Group Discussion on January 26, 2018).

In somewhat a different viewpoint, Arif said the reason for other claimant states not pursuing a similar arbitration route was because other countries are economically dependent on China. In fact, all regional countries – claimant as well as non-claimant states – want to have cordial relations with China. At the same time, they are wary of China's dominance in the region, so they want the US to back them up. In case of the Philippines, domestic politics came into play. Duterte thought it was necessary to reestablish ties with China so that it can use its financial assistance to fight drug problems, terrorism, and for infrastructural development and so forth (Interview on January 22, 2018). In somewhat similar analysis, Kembara said other claimants do not have the US behind them like the Philippines. They thought that had a situation rose to a conflict with China, they would not have major powers to help them. The other reason is because of China's economic leverage. One example is China's large investment in Malaysia. Had Malaysia taken the same route, it could have lost major economic assistance. The Philippines lost economic assistance from China when they approached the PCA, but things changed when Duterte came to power. Also, some countries in ASEAN will not like to support either party but rather to stay in the sideline (Interview on January 18, 2018).

Looking from the legal perspective, Tseng said the legal route is not the priority for other claimant states. In other words, they don't want to enter into a legal battle with China. The other reason is that the arbitral ruling did not make any significant change or progress on the issue. The only other claimant which would pursue a legal course is Vietnam, but both China and Vietnam share a similar view on law, that is, to promote social harmony. Other claimant states also feel that taking China to the arbitration court will significantly reduce the room for bilateral negotiation. The current Vietnamese leaders are largely pro-China. Also, since there is also a significant Chinese population in Vietnam, the government feels the need to maintain good relations with China. No significant change is expected even if a new party or leadership comes to power, at least in the next few years (2–3 years). But the new leadership may raise the need for a multilateral forum such as ASEAN. Most countries in the international community will not argue with China when it says that Taiwan is an integral part of China. Involving Taiwan in the SCS issue is helpful for ASEAN claimant states because it will have another friend. However, China would not discuss the issue of Taiwan's involvement. Vietnam is the only country which wants Taiwan's issue as a bargaining leverage. The problem, however, is that Taiwan does not have the necessary power to defend its SCS claim against the threat of China. Thus, Taiwan should not intervene in the dispute since there is no consensus for its participation. After all, the claims of China and Taiwan are more or less the same. And apparently after 2014, China seems to be willing to use force against Taiwan if necessary. Brunei does not occupy any islands, so it is better for it to stay that way (stay low). What Brunei wants is resource sharing. Malaysia maintains a low profile in order to receive Chinese economic investment (Interview on December 19, 2017).

Along similar line, Beckman, a leading legal scholar on the issue, said, first, it is because China ignored the ruling. Second, the parties are still waiting to see what happens. The other claimants do not want to spend millions of dollars to bring China to the court. They are neither willing nor have the capacity to confront China. China has restrained itself in the dispute to some extent after the ruling, not to aggravate the situation. The other claimants are aware that China does not want another arbitration but rather to pursue cooperation with other states (Interview on December 15, 2017). However, another legal scholar, Ariadno, said the reason why other claimants are not pursuing the arbitration route is that within ASEAN, there are supporters of China as well as states that are against. Also, there is a neutral party like Indonesia. ASEAN cannot reach a consensus on the issue. The arbitration can be cited for other similar cases. For example, Indonesia can refer to the arbitral ruling with respect to the case of the Natuna Islands. Somehow, China is trying to respond to the arbitral ruling with its new concept of the One Belt One Road initiative. I do not believe China is completely ignoring the UNCLOS ruling. The country is being influenced or cornered, and maybe they also feel insecure. But I do not know if they try to honor or follow international law. China is using the Belt and Road Initiative to take the pressure off the arbitral ruling. The ruling is also a legal source for members of the international community (Interview on January 25, 2018).

A Vietnamese scholar, Hiep, said that first, the ruling is applicable mainly to the dispute between China and the Philippines. For Brunei and Malaysia, they have no political and economic reasons to take a similar approach, and moreover, they are benefiting from China's trade and investment. In fact, all other claimant states are benefiting from the Philippines petition. If Vietnam wants to file, it can file a similar case on the Paracels, but it does not choose that partly because there have been strong communist party-to-party ties and Vietnam also receives huge economic benefits from China. But Vietnam still has an option to do that at some point if they are not happy with the situation. Taiwan has more or less the same position with China, as well as the same national sentiment over the dispute. Also, Taiwan will not challenge any claims made by China (Interview on December 22, 2017). Echoing the same view, another scholar, Chalermpalanupap, said Vietnam considered taking China to the arbitration court on the Paracels but thought it was not necessary since the ruling on the Philippines' case offered sufficient evidence. Moreover, China had been immensely humiliated, and Vietnam does not want to make it worse (Interview on December 22, 2017).

Somewhat drifting from others, Lean said other claimant states do not have to pursue the arbitration route for the simple fact that various ASEAN members blamed the Philippines for sidestepping them, not for consulting them or bringing them into the dispute. The ASEAN claimant states, particularly Vietnam, believe that the arbitration has resolved the fundamental problem of the SCS disputes. They do not see the need to do a double job. Duterte does not say that the arbitral ruling is not valid, but he wants to set it aside for now and use it later at an appropriate time. Other ASEAN claimant states see that the arbitration is also applicable to their individual cases. Eventually if they want to pursue the legal course, they can use the arbitral ruling as the basis for discussion and negotiation. The award does not resolve the sovereignty issue. The arbitration says that none of the features in the SCS is an island. They are basically rocks, low tide elevation or shoals. After the arbitration ruling, China has recalibrated its strategy on how they look at the Nine-Dash Line with a new thinking of four sha, a possible policy of China which came up recently this year, though they still officially maintain the Nine-Dash Line claim. The most important dispute in the SCS is in the Spratlys, which is a multilateral dispute. The Paracels is a dispute only between China and Vietnam. China would have to find a solution first with Taiwan, especially on the one-China policy, because Taiwan seems to be unwilling to support China's claims even though Beijing wants them to (Interview on December 26, 2017).

Hongzhou said that, on paper, the ruling was considered a huge win for the Philippines, but that the question is how much can the ruling be implemented? What can it change on the ground? There is no sign that China would accept it. Vietnam was also initially thinking of pursuing the case through arbitration but dropped the idea. For them, communist party-to-party ties are important in their relations. No country in Southeast Asia, including the claimant states, is willing to endanger or damage its bilateral relations with China, which is a major power in the region. Even for the Philippines, its relations with China were cut off right after the arbitration but were repaired or resumed after Duterte came to power. The entire arbitration process lasted four years. The US is far away and China is a major neighbor power. How can a small country in the region live in strained ties with China? This is not pragmatic. We should be realistic; what can Taiwan really do here when it cannot even participate in formal international meetings as a sovereign power or active claimant? Malaysia has been exploiting oil and gas resources and developing it for many years within the Nine-Dash Line, but China has not taken any major action on this, and maybe this is why it has been quiet. Malaysia's general population doesn't seem to care about the SCS issue. As Brunei is a small country, there is no need for it to make noise. China has neither harassed nor made any threatening move toward it, plus Brunei largely depends on China for its oil market. For Indonesia, there is an internal conflict in terms of budget as the navy in the defense ministry is fighting for it. Their EEZ overlap with China's Nine-Dash Line, but the Indonesian navy and coast guards have taken bribes and allowed the Chinese fishermen to fish in their EEZ. The Natuna Island incident began in March 2016 when the Indonesian coast guards captured the Chinese ship and arrested nine fishermen. When Chinese coast guards came to their rescue, it took more than 10 hours and they entered beyond the Nine-Dash Line and a few miles from Natuna Island. It was a threat from the Indonesian law enforcement perspective, but for China their fishermen were there fishing for many years but no severe actions had been taken and they questioned why such actions were being taken now. China sent its envoys to Indonesia to settle the matter, which was a big issue in Indonesia. Each country's domestic politics plays an important role in the SCS disputes (Interview on December 20, 2017).

Conclusion

It is clear from the existing literature, as well as from the views expressed by experts and people who are directly or indirectly affected by the tribunal ruling, that there is no consensus strategy on the issue before and after arbitration. Now the lingering question is what should the international community do if China continues to ignore the arbitral ruling. For example, should the US, EU, ASEAN, any other international organization(s) or the other claimant states step up their pressure on China to respect the tribunal's ruling? But that will not seem to bring any significant change, at least in the near future. If China continues to maintain its intransigence, then what should the international community do? These answers appear bleak, since the tribunal ruling was largely symbolic given China's reluctance to fulfill its international obligation. But what is clear from the arbitration is that China's claim over the Nine-Dash Line has no legal basis. And the ruling can now serve as the foundation for other claimants. The bottom line is that all claimants have varying levels of interests and priorities. Despite the heightened tension between the Philippines and China over the ruling, the status quo on the SCS has not changed significantly. Moreover, other domestic priorities of the Duterte administration have emphasized improving ties with China, especially economic aid and infrastructural development assistance.

5 The role of the United States and others

China strongly rejected the tribunal ruling, but countries such as the US, Australia, Japan, India, and New Zealand urged both parties to respect the ruling and restraint from provocative activities (The Philippine Star 2016). The international community is visibly divided on the issue. While support for the Philippines's position came mostly from Western countries and Asia, Beijing found its supporters from nations mostly in Africa and the Middle East. Though the US has not ratified the UNCLOS, it wants China to respect the international law. Since the tribunal ruling has no enforcement power, its impact largely depends on the reaction of the international community. The Philippines has the support of the EU and the G-7 nations. Australia and India are two other countries supportive of the application and respect for international law. On the other hand, China has claimed that it has the support of countries such as Afghanistan, The Gambia, Niger, Sudan and Vanuatu, as well as the 21-member Arab League.

For many political analysts, the tension in the SCS is about geopolitics or power rivalry of great powers, especially between China and the US. The SCS has integrated into the Chinese strategic rivalry with the US ever since China became a major naval power and its subsequent deployments (Buszynski 2012). China's increasing assertiveness in the region and the US attempts to counterbalance it are a manifestation of great power rivalry. Unsurprisingly, China has been increasingly more concerned with the US naval activity in the SCS than the efforts of other claimant states or a collective engagement of ASEAN as an organization. Rising China's quest for influence in East Asia has questioned the status of the US as a superpower in the region (Cronin and Kaplan 2012). More importantly, the rise of China came at a time when there was a generalized crisis for the US leadership globally (Rolf and Agnew 2016).

The US, Japan, Australia and several other countries in the region have expressed concerns over the significant growth of the Chinese defense budget and the lack of transparency behind the rational for such massive expenditure. While the actual defense budget is believed to be much higher than what is officially stated, its defense spending has increased more than 500 percent since 1997, where the defense spending exceeded the economic spending. The US has been particularly concerned about the Chinese military buildup, which it believes is more than a defensive purpose (Thayer 2010).

US policy toward the South China Sea

The role of US has become increasingly important. Washington's policy toward the SCS can be broadly discussed under four principles: a peaceful resolution of the issue by the concerned states that enhances regional peace, prosperity and security; opposition to the threat or use of force to assert any claims in the SCS; maintaining neutrality on the merits of competing sovereignty claims and willing to help in the peaceful resolution of the disputes; and maintaining lines of communication in the region and resisting any maritime claims beyond those permitted by the UNCLOS. Nevertheless, the primary interest of the US government is freedom of navigation, and although it does not ratify the UNCLOS, it wants all claimants, including China, to respect the tribunal's verdict. The other reason, which has not been explicitly stated or advocated, is Washington's strategic calculation, which is largely seen by Beijing as America's containment policy in the region. The continued US navy presence and the drills it has carried out in the SCS and China's assertive stance to protect its maritime claims within the Nine-Dash Line are signs of a precarious future. The simmering situation escalated when the Chinese and Russian naval forces conducted an eight-day joint exercise in the SCS involving "live-fire drills, sea crossing and island landing operations, and island defense and offense exercises" in mid-September 2016 (Lendon and Hunt 2016).

Since the end of Cold War, the US policy on the SCS has been largely reactive. The US took a first public position in late 1994 when China occupied the Mischief Reef. With the growing concern for stability in the SCS region, the US State Department issued a statement in May 1995: it strongly opposed the use or threat of force to resolve the competing claims; it called upon claimants to intensify diplomatic efforts to address the issues involved; it declared its willingness to assist in any way deemed helpful; it welcomed and supported the 1992 ASEAN Declaration of the South China Sea; it emphasized that "unhindered navigation by all ships and aircraft in the South China Sea is essential for the peace and prosperity of the entire Asia Pacific region, including the United States"; and it took no position on the legal merits of the claims. However, it would view "with serious concern any maritime claims, or restriction on maritime activity, in the South China Sea that was not consistent with international law, including the 1982 United Nations Convention on the Law of the Sea" (To 2003, 33).

From the US perspective, all countries should equally have access to and enjoy freedom in the high seas, including Freedom of Navigation Operations (FONOPs) beyond a coastal state's 12 nautical miles of territorial sea over which it enjoys sovereign rights. Commercial as well as military vessels should enjoy high seas freedom in accordance with Articles 56 and 87 of the UNCLOS. In line with this assertion, the US has conducted multiple operational assertions in the waters of Malaysia, Vietnam and China since 2007. Unhindered access to the waters in the SCS is mainly important for two reasons. First are concerns with the economic dynamism of the region, which involves intra-regional and international trade amounting to more than $5 trillion of trade passing through these waters, including more than $1 trillion with the US. Unhindered access to the waters is also important for the US to project its military power, not just in East Asia but across the globe. Many US naval vessels from the West Coast and Japan pass through the SCS en route to the Indian Ocean and Persian Gulf. And the US wants to maintain the principle of freedom of navigation around the world. But the US insistence on unhindered access to the SCS has met with challenges. One major challenge is the Chinese interpretation of coastal states' EEZs, especially since the EP-3 incident on April 1, 2001, when a US Navy EP-3E ARIES II signals intelligence aircraft and China's PLAN J-8II interceptor fighter jet collided in mid-air, which resulted in an international dispute between the two countries. Since then, China has flouted several legal arguments with the aim to limit US surveillance and reconnaissance activities. The second is the modernization of PLA-N, which can eventually have the potential to neutralize the US vessels from these waters. The US also has a significant interest in the maintenance of regional peace and stability in Southeast Asia, which is important for trade and cross-border investment across the region (Fravel 2014).

The US made a renewed interest in the SCS during the Obama administration. The gravity of the US policy on the SCS was evidenced from Obama's Asian pivot agenda (Rolf and Agnew 2016). In early March 2009, the Obama administration sent two senior officials to Beijing and were received by Chinese State Councilor Dai Bingguo. The two visiting officials were told by their counterparts, among others, that "China would not tolerate any interference in the South China Sea, now part of China's 'core interest' of sovereignty." This was the first time China had identified the SCS as a core interest, along with Tibet, Taiwan and Xinjiang (Thayer 2011c, 17). By 2009, it was evident that the US paid closer attention on the SCS, particularly for two reasons. The first was due to Chinese threats to the US oil companies operating off the coast of Vietnam in 2008, which was the first direct challenge to the US commercial interest and US companies by China in the SCS. The second was because of the Chinese harassment of the USNS *Impeccable* and other US naval surveillance vessels during their FONOPS in the high seas. By 2010, the Obama administration felt the need for a new policy on the SCS. During the July 2010 annual meeting of the ARF, the US and 12 other countries expressed concerns over the rising tensions in the SCS. US Secretary of State Hillary Clinton affirmed the 1995 policy in a public statement on the US position, including freedom of navigation, opposition to the use or threat of force by any claimant and the US refraining from taking any side in the competing territorial claims. She also introduced new policies that were not part of the 1995 statement: resolving disputes without coercion; support for a "collaborative diplomatic process by all claimants," including a willingness to "facilitate initiatives and confidence building measures consistent with the [2002 Declaration on a Code of Conduct]"; support for drafting of a full code of conduct; and the position that "legitimate claims to maritime space in the South China Sea should be derived solely from legitimate claims to land features" (Fravel 2014, 4–5).

In recent years, the US criticism of the Chinese position on the SCS has seemingly shifted from freedom of navigation to the larger question of international law or norms. For example, in August 2014, US Secretary of State John Kerry said that tensions in the SCS are "more than claims to islands and reefs and rocks and the economic interests that flow from them. They're about whether might makes right or whether global rules and norms and rule of law and international law will prevail." The emphasis on international law was also evidenced with the US support for the Philippines' case against China at The Hague, with the US State Department spokeswoman saying, "We hope that this case serves to provide greater legal certainty and compliance with the international law of the sea" (Roy 2016, 239). Interestingly, President Donald Trump had offered to mediate on the SCS. During his visit to Hanoi, Vietnam, on November 12, 2017, at the start of a meeting with the Vietnamese President Tran Dai Quang, Trump said, while acknowledging that China's position on the SCS issue was a problem, "If I can help mediate or arbitrate, please let me know. . . . I'm a very good mediator and arbitrator" (Holland, Chalmers and Gopalakrishnan 2017).

After China and ASEAN agreed on a single text to negotiate the COC in the SCS on August 2, 2018, the US reiterated its emphasis on international norms. US Ambassador Piper Campbell, charge d'affaires at the US Mission to ASEAN, said,

> It's important that all countries, regardless of their size, have the opportunity to represent their national interests as well as the very clear international principles including the principles that are enshrined in [the Law of the Sea]. That position is unchanged.

She also said forums such as the EAS provide a good opportunity for the US to discuss the SCS issue with its Asian partners, and added:

> Those meetings in Singapore provided an excellent opportunity for frank and clear conversations on the situation in the South China Sea, and to raise our very real concerns about ongoing activities of militarization and to ask for clarity about how those actual steps on the ground, how those fit with the principles that were enumerated by almost every country in the discussion.

Moreover, during an interview with Voice of America, Chief of Naval Operations Admiral John Richardson said the US response to China's controversial actions in the SCS maintains " 'consistency' and it has been 'at about the same force levels' for about 70 years. . . . Nothing has elevated too much or decreased too much. We've been pretty steady" (Khemara 2018). Besides the publicly stated freedom of navigation, US naval operations are targeting what the US believes to be excessive claims about maritime boundaries and jurisdiction over airspace above its EEZ, challenging China's domestic law criminalizing foreign survey activities in its EEZ, and also because of the Chinese insistence of obtaining permission before passing through its territorial seas (Glaser 2014, 57)

While it is not opposed to the COC discussion between China and ASEAN, Randall Schriver, US Assistant Secretary of Defense for Indo-Pacific Security Affairs, questioned the motive of China on April 26, 2019, and said, "We do have some suspicion about China's motive. . . . The way they behave suggests that they are not participant in upholding international law consistently . . . So we would have suspicion in terms of what they seek in the code of conduct." He further said that the US would like ASEAN to pursue a legally binding code that would govern the actions of all claimant states in the SCS and would be "consistent with existing international laws and norms." The comments were made two days after China displayed its first aircraft carrier, the *Liaoning*, during a naval review off the coast of northern port city of Qingdao. In the exercise, more than 30 Chinese boats, submarines and frigates and almost 40 warplanes took part. The strong display, which marked the Chinese navy's 70th anniversary, was part of a major public relations drive by its military amid rising concerns over its activities in the SCS, where it has built military installations atop seven man-made islands it occupies. In his speech after the military show on April 24, 2019, the Chinese navy chief Shen Jinlong said that freedom of navigation should not be used to violate the rights of other countries (BenarNews 2019). Earlier on March 8, 2019, the Chinese state-run *China Daily* quoted Chinese Foreign Minister Wang Yi, who said that the talk on COC will speed up and should be ready for signature by 2020, ahead of China's previous forecast of 2021 (Jennings 2019).

India and the South China Sea

India is not a claimant in the SCS but has stakes when it comes to geopolitics, geo-strategy and geo-economics. Geographically, India is not in the SCS region but it is involved in the region with the littoral states through naval exercises and visits, strategic partnerships and oil exploration as well as through diplomatic channels at multilateral forums. India has engaged countries in the SCS region in line with what it calls an "extended neighborhood" since the concept was first used in 2000. The goal was to move beyond countries in South Asia, which are vital for its strategic and economic objectives (Jawli 2016). In the past two decades or so, ASEAN and East Asia have formed the fastest growing regions for India's economic and strategic interests (Puri and Sahgal 2011). But when India established ties with ASEAN in the early 1990s, security was not a priority. While the ASEAN leaders were ready to experiment economic ties with India, they were wary of security entanglement. When the ARF was formed, initially ASEAN did not want India to apply for membership. And when it did apply, the application was rejected. The ASEAN leaders were worried that India would bring its difficult security matters with Pakistan and China to the forum. And when India was admitted to ARF in 1997, there was an understanding that India would maintain low-key status until the economic relationship took momentum before security and political issues can be discussed. And in fact, India's initial goal was to focus on economic and institutional partnership (Mohan 2008). In an attempt to further strengthen ties with the ASEAN individual countries, India forged ties with Cambodia, Laos, Myanmar, and Vietnam (CLMV), which supported the idea of India holding a summit-level dialogue with ASEAN. In 1997, India expanded its regional ties by forming the Bangladesh-India-Sri Lanka-Thailand Economic Cooperation (BISTEC) with countries in South Asia and Southeast Asia: Bangladesh, India, Sri Lanka, Thailand, Nepal and Bhutan. After Myanmar joined the organization, it was changed to the Bay of Bengal Initiative for Multi-Sectoral Technical and Economic Cooperation (BIMSTEC). The primary goal was to create a free trade zone among member states before 2017 (Hong 2007).

Gradually, India has expanded its relationship with both ASEAN and the larger Asia Pacific region. Today, India has maintained its naval presence in the SCS for almost two decades. The types of deployment include movement of the Indian navy, bilateral exercises, port calls to friendly nations and transit through the waters. Regarding the UNCLOS tribunal ruling on the SCS disputes, New Delhi called for self-restraint on all parties and to abide by international law (Chaudhury 2018). India's official policy on the SCS was stated by the Minister of State for External Affairs, General V.K. Singh, in the Upper House of the Indian Parliament on August 4, 2016 when he said that India

> supports freedom of navigation and over flight, and unimpeded commerce, based on the principles of international law, as reflected notably in the UNCLOS. India believes that States should resolve disputes through peaceful means without threat or use of force and exercise self-restraint in the conduct of activities that could complicate or escalate disputes affecting peace and stability. As a State Party to the UNCLOS, India urges all parties to show utmost respect for the UNCLOS, which establishes the international legal order of the seas and oceans.
>
> (Jawli 2016)

The Act East Policy (AEP), which was introduced as the Look East Policy (LEP) in 1991, was aimed at reaching out to Southeast Asia and East Asia. Part of the AEP is to gain preeminent status in the Indian Ocean, as well as to contain or counterbalance the growing influence of China in the region, including the SCS. India is wary of China having complete control of the SCS, which would then bring their maritime forces to the Strait of Malacca choke point, close to the Indian Ocean, which is an entry point to India's backyard. India does not want that to happen. The SCS region is also important for India since it lies at the intervening stretch of waters between the Indian Ocean and the western Pacific. As the maritime cooperation with the US and Australia continues to grow, the waters have been referred to as the Indo-Pacific by these countries. The Indian navy also operates in the western Pacific in cooperation with the navies of the US and Japan, and therefore, it is even more important for India to have a secure passage in the SCS. In other words, for India to navigate peacefully from the Indian Ocean to the western Pacific, unhindered access to the SCS is essential.

While India and the US share similar interests on freedom of navigation and/or compliance with international law, India does not share the notion of conducting maritime operations in the SCS to score "political points," nor would India publicly support the US strategy in the region that would justify China's greater maritime activities near the Andaman Islands. Given this sensitive possible repercussion, India and the US may not engage in joint patrols in the SCS, at least in the near future, although New Delhi supports Washington's position on territorial disputes (Singh 2016a). While it may not take sides on the SCS dispute, China's increasing assertiveness and its maritime activities in India's own backyard may entail India strengthening its naval presence in the region (Singh 2016b).

It is clear that India has gradually improved ties with countries in Southeast and East Asia over the years. This is evident from the fact that India has taken policy initiatives in the region that involve some members of ASEAN, such as BIMSTEC, the Mekong-Ganga Cooperation and so forth. Moreover, India is an active participant in several regional forums such as the Asia-Europe Meeting (ASEM), EAS, ARF, ADMM Plus and Expanded ASEAN Maritime Forum (EAMF). But when it comes to the SCS dispute, India urges countries to respect the UNCLOS. New Delhi has taken a principled stance on the SCS issue and its eastern outreach in the wake of the July 12, 2016, arbitral ruling that challenged China's territorial and maritime claims. India supports freedom of navigation and overflight, and unimpeded commerce, based on the principles of international law as reflected in UNCLOS. India also strongly believes that states should resolve disputes through peaceful means without threat or use of force and should exercise self-restraint in the conduct of activities that could complicate or escalate disputes affecting peace and stability.

The India-ASEAN relationship, or even with the East Asian countries, will continue to grow in the future, but for India the relationship is more geared toward economic benefits than any other objectives or issues. Therefore, it is unlikely that New Delhi will take any concrete or confrontational step(s) that could escalate tensions with China. So long as India is hesitant or reluctant to speak out on the assertive or aggressive activities of China, ASEAN members will continue to view India as an unreliable security partner.

Australia and the South China Sea

Although Australia is not a member of ASEAN, it became a dialogue partner in 1974 and it was a founding member of ARF in 1994. Australia is also a participant in all of the security forums such as EAS and the ADMM Plus, thereby giving it an important multilateral forum to play a constructive role in the region (Lee 2013). Since the past several decades, Australia has made public statements on the territorial disputes of the SCS but has not taken a side on the issue. A 2016 white paper clearly indicated that Australia's defense strategy in the SCS is driven by three interests: a secure, resilient Australia, with secure northern approaches and proximate sea lines of communication; a secure nearer region, encompassing maritime Southeast Asia and the South Pacific; and a stable Indo-Pacific region and a rules-based global order. These stated strategic interests have been maintained consistently for more than half a century. On the military significance of the SCS, Australia's Joint Intelligence Committee gave a briefing in 1959 which stated:

> On 27th April 1950, in connection with the formation of a draft peace treaty with Japan, the Defense Committee agreed that it was in Australia's strategic interests to work for U.S. Trusteeship of the Spratly Islands. In fact, the Peace Treaty left the question of sovereignty unsettled. In May 1950, Australia was concerned, for strategic reasons, that the Spratly Islands might fall into Chinese Communist hands. In an attempt to forestall this, the United Kingdom was sounded out about accepting trusteeship of the islands. The United Kingdom replied that they would probably be unwilling to do anything which would embarrass them in relations with the Communist Chinese. They foresaw the danger their occupation of the islands might be resisted. If, in the longer term, the Communist Chinese were to develop the islands militarily, they could make a nuisance out of themselves on the international shipping and air routes on the pretext of infringements of territorial waters and air space and might even shoot down an aircraft occasionally. Again, there is little the West is likely to do, except protest.
>
> (Brennan 2017)

But in recent years, the Australian position has been questioned or even undermined particularly by the Chinese assertiveness and its expansionist moves, such as land reclamation and the construction of artificial islands. This was compounded by the fact that China refused to participate and acknowledge the arbitration proceedings under the UNCLOS. Faced with new uncertainties, Australia felt the need for building a coalition with its ASEAN partners. In March 2018, ahead of its special meeting with ASEAN states, Australian Foreign Minister Julie Bishop emphasized the need for international law to prevail. In a leaked draft of the speech, Bishop said "the rules-based order is designed to regulate behavior and rivalries of and between states, and ensure countries compete fairly and in a way that does not threaten others or destabilizes their region or the world." She added that "it places limitations on the extent to which countries use their economic or military power to impose unfair agreements on less powerful nations" (Packham 2018). A few months later, on July 12, 2018, Australian Defence Minister Kevin Andrews strongly opposed the Chinese "intimidation and aggression" in the disputed SCS, and he added that

> Territorial disputes continue to risk regional stability and create uncertainty. One issue that has attracted a lot of international attention in recent months is the South China Sea. Australia has a legitimate interest in the maintenance of peace and stability, respect for international law, unimpeded trade and freedom of navigation and overflight in the South China Sea.
>
> (Press Trust of India (PTI) 2018a)

In late May 2019, Australia-China relations were visibly strained when Australian navy helicopter pilots who were conducting a military exercise in the SCS were hit with laser beams, allegedly by passing Chinese fishing boats. As a result, some pilots were grounded for precautionary medical reasons. This was reportedly the first time the Australian military had been targeted by lasers. Moreover, the Australians were apparently followed at a distance by a Chinese warship, although they were not close to any of the features occupied by the Chinese forces (Martin 2019). The Chinese Defense Ministry angrily responded to the Australian claims, and its spokesman Wu Qian said the claims were "not consistent with the facts" (Withers 2019).

Japan and the South China Sea

Like India and Australia, Japan is also not a claimant but has had a presence in the SCS for years. A Japanese company began mining in the Spratly Islands in 1918, and in the 1920s several Japanese companies occupied various islands and excavated guano for fertilizer. And in February 1939, the Japanese forces occupied the large island of Hainan in Southern China and the Paracel Islands, where they established a submarine base at Itu Aba or Taiping Island (Rowan 2005). But after its defeat in World War II, Japan was forced to give up its occupied territories including Formosa (now Taiwan), the Pescadores and the Spratly and Paracel Islands. In the post–Cold War era, Japan renewed its interest in the SCS for specific reasons. The first is that Japanese vessels use the SCS sea lanes to carry 70 percent of its oil. Though Japan can avoid any potential conflict by sailing around Indonesia into the Pacific Ocean, that would be more costly and time-consuming. The second reason is that Japan wants to expand its influence in East Asia. Third, Tokyo is visibly concerned about the Chinese creeping influence and assertiveness in Asia, particularly the SCS. Japan has tried to use two common platforms to address the SCS disputes. First is through the ARF, where both Japan and China are members. The second is through promoting the workshops on the SCS organized annually by Indonesia (Rowan 2005). Since the late 2000s, Japan has made efforts to participate in multilateral gatherings to emphasize the importance of freedom of navigation based on the rule of law, and has supported the position of US and ASEAN to find a peaceful resolution to the SCS disputes. Japan has also established bilateral ties with the ASEAN claimants, particularly Vietnam and the Philippines (Shoji 2014).

But in the last two decades, especially after 2010, Japan's presence in the SCS is closely connected to its own maritime dispute with China. Japan confronted China over territorial disputes in the Senkaku/Diaoyu Islands in the East China Sea. For example, in September 2010, the Japanese coast guard arrested a Chinese fishing boat and crew members who were charged with illegally operating in the Japanese waters and obstructing the Japanese coast guards from performing their duties. China reacted strongly to the incident, which led to serious diplomatic tensions between the two countries. Two years later, Japan nationalized three of the privately-owned islands. Tensions consequently escalated and the Chinese responded by locking fire-control radar on the Maritime Self-Defense Force destroyer in January 2013; in November of that same year, China also imposed the East China Sea Air Defence Identification Zone. For Japan, there is a strong connection between the Chinese activities in the East China Sea and the SCS, that is, the denial of activities to foreign navies and acquiring Chinese navy access to the western Pacific. For Japan, they believe that the Chinese maritime or military strategy toward other claimants in the SCS would be enforced in a similar manner toward Japan. In case China succeeds in convincing or coercing the other SCS claimants to accept its historical rights claim, this would not only undermine international norms but also have a serious impact on the East China Sea dispute (Yoshimatsu 2017).

The Japanese position on the SCS is also more or less similar to the US and Australia. A couple of days after the July 2016 arbitration, the Japanese Foreign Ministry Spokesman Yasuhisa Kawamura said Prime Minister Shinzo Abe reiterated the fundamental position of Japan in the SCS during his meeting with Chinese Premier Li Keqiang on the sidelines of the ASEM Summit in Ulaanbaatar, Mongolia, on July 15, 2016, that "The situation of the South China Sea is the concern of the international community. The tribunal award of 12 July is final and legally binding on the parties to the dispute," and therefore, rules-based international order should be respected. In response, the Chinese Premier Li Keqiang reportedly said that "Japan is not a state directly involved in the South China Sea issue, and thus should exercise caution in its own words and deeds, and stop hyping up and interfering" (Wong and Edwards 2016).

Though Japan intends to protect its interest in the SCS, as well as the East China Sea, its military and naval powers are incapable of doing so on its own. This is why its security alliance with the US is quite important, including joint frequent military drills (Johnson 2019). There are analysts, including those from Japan, who argue that Washington is the only potential game-changer in the SCS, that is, to stop or prevent China from its aggressive and expansionist moves. In fact, no coastal states in the SCS can match the maritime powers of China. In 2014, a Japanese Vice Admiral (Retired) Japan Maritime Self Defense Force wrote:

> The only possible measure to make up for this handicap is U.S. forces' capability to destroy China's major infrastructures and military facilities in the region. . . . China's major bases, such as Sanya, Woody Island, Johnson South Reef, and perhaps Scarborough Shoal in the future, have huge strategic significance; however, they are also subject to vulnerabilities in their base protection, especially that from incoming precision-guided missiles. Since all of these key bases expose themselves to external sea and air space, they will become easy targets of U.S. long-range Tomahawks and air-launched cruise missiles. If the United States intends to employ swarm attack tactics, it would be impossible for China to protect these bases from these serious threats. In this point of view, Washington, D.C., should send a clear signal to Beijing that the United States is determined to exercise this capability when necessary, and to deter China's adventurism in the South China Sea. This will be a real contribution provided by the United States and its forces, which coastal states have long awaited.
>
> (Koda 2014, 95)

Quadrilateral Security Dialogue

The Quadrilateral Security Dialogue (QSD or the Quad) is an informal strategic dialogue between the US, Japan, Australia and India that was initially initiated in 2007 by Prime Minister Shinzo Abe of Japan, with the support of Vice President Dick Cheney of the US, Prime Minister John Howard of Australia and Prime Minister Manmohan Singh of India. The security dialogue between the countries was followed by joint military exercises of an unprecedented scale, titled Exercise Malabar. The Quad formation was widely viewed as a response to increased Chinese economic and military power. The Quad ceased to function following the withdrawal of Australia. But the quadrilateral alliance was revived during the 2017 ASEAN Summits in Manila by Prime Minister Malcolm Turnbull of Australia, Prime Minister Shinzo Abe of Japan, Prime Minister Narendra Modi of India and President Donald Trump of the US amidst the rising tensions in the SCS due to China's increasing assertiveness and territorial ambitions. The security pact was revived to develop a strategy to keep critical sea routes in the Indo-Pacific free of anyone's influence. The US has been pushing India to take a much greater role, which is viewed largely to contain the rising China. However, India has been reluctant to give a military shape to the Quad formation (Press Trust of India 2018c).

Undoubtedly, India could play a more active role, but it is clear that New Delhi does not want to drag itself into the great power rivalry game of the US and China in the Indo-Pacific region. In other words, India does not want to be seen as either an ally of the US or China. There are criticisms about the ineffectiveness or powerlessness of the Quad. Some suggest that for the security pact to become more effective, it needs to expand dialogue partners by including the ASEAN maritime claimant states. Unless there are participants from the ASEAN claimant states, the Quad is widely viewed as a tool of the West to contain China. The Quad can also engage in a track-1.5 discussions, thereby involving government officials and other experts to discuss the mutual concern of all members. For example, with its increasing military capability and good relationships with the entire Quad members, Vietnam can be a potential new member (Grossman 2018). As one Indian journalist suggested in her analysis in the *Pioneer* newspaper, a strengthened Quad could be helpful to "maintain international law, ensure peaceful settlement of disputes and freedom of navigation and allow commerce in the region, including the South China sea, according to global practices" (Singh 2019).

A more critical analysis of the Quad is the differences over the concept itself by member states which one scholar puts it:

> For India Indo-Pacific includes the whole Indian Ocean from Africa to the US. For Australia it stops at Bay of Bengal. Japan has no problem with India's narrative. And the US says it is a geopolitical imagination. The problem here is that this Indo-Pacific construct is still not supported by a multilateral institution. So no one is clear about the duties, responsibilities and benefits. There needs to be a clear blueprint for the Quad.
>
> (The Times of India 2018)

Another analyst goes to the point saying that the formation of the Quad should not be seen as an alliance against China. India takes a principled position on the SCS and supports ASEAN centrality and peaceful settlement of disputes between claimant states (Interview on December 21, 2017). And yet some are optimistic that while members are still in the process of defining their priorities, there have been some structural changes in the Indo-Pacific region over the past few years because of China's rise and its behavior (Pant and Bommakanti 2018). In a new development, the Quad was elevated to a ministerial level dialogue on September 27, 2019, in New York, which was attended by US Secretary of State Mike Pompeo, Indian External Affairs Minister S. Jaishankar, and Foreign Ministers Toshimitsu Motegi of Japan and Marise Payne of Australia. Following the meeting, the US Acting Assistant Secretary for South Asia Alice Wells said at a State Department briefing: "We had a wide-ranging discussion of our collective efforts to advance a free and open Indo-Pacific, but also touching on counterterrorism, humanitarian assistance and disaster relief, maritime security cooperation, development finance, and cybersecurity." But despite the elevation to a ministerial level, the group wants to maintain a low profile and not making it a military alliance (IANS 2019).

Should the US play a more active role?

Given the nature of geopolitics or the great power rivalry in the SCS, the question is whether the US should play a more active or greater role as a power balancer? If so, how? Unsurprisingly, opinions are divided among observers and scholars on the issue. Tran said the US has been active with national defense strategy and national security strategy. The US is still here in the region. The dispute has to be resolved by the claimant states. The US calls for upholding and respect for international law. The US may not ratify, but it upholds and adheres to the rules and regulations under UNCLOS. On the other hand, China ratifies the UNCLOS but does not respect the arbitral ruling. What the US calls for are freedom of navigation and peaceful resolution of the disputes. The US has its presence in the region both militarily and economically and it will continue to maintain that way. During the Obama administration, it was pivot-Asia and during the Trump administration it is Indo-Pacific policy. In terms of foreign policy, there may be different statements but the fundamental policy of the US remains the same. There is always a concern for military conflict on the ground. For example, though China says it wants to resolve the issue peacefully, their actions do not say that. For the US, it is about settlement of the disputes peacefully. The US has raised the SCS issue with China and other states in the region, including Indonesia (Interview on January 26, 2018).

For Kraft, there is a difference between what the countries in the region expect the US to do. The US has said that freedom of navigation cannot be violated by China's claims, but at the same time the US records on the issue has been mixed. President Obama was relatively more engaged on the issue and President Trump is unpredictable. Meanwhile, President Duterte is willing to throw away its traditional relationship with the US, which no other administration has ever done (Interview on November 29, 2017). Carpio said the US has already said it will not take a side in territorial disputes, which means that China will go ahead with its activities. China believes that the US will not stop them, although the Philippines has defense treaty with the US. Moreover, the US has never said that it will defend the Scarborough Shoal (Interview on December 8, 2017).

Banlaoi said, in the region, there is a general agreement of not involving external powers. During the Aquino government, the Philippines involved the US but Duterte said the issue can be resolved bilaterally by China and the Philippines. The US says that they are the Asian Pacific power but they do not use it to balance China; their words do not match their actions. There was dissatisfaction from the Philippines; the US could have prevented the Chinese artificial island buildings but they did not stop it. ASEAN does not want to be in a position where it is forced to choose one party or the other, that is, the US or China (Interview on December 5, 2017).

In somewhat a positive tone, Baviera said the US has always played a consistent role but it has been largely symbolic, focusing mainly on freedom of navigation. However, its position is not enough to balance China. The US will not do more than what it has already done in case China occupies the SCS militarily because the US needs China on the Korean peninsula crisis. What the US should do is not military action or building military coalitions but rather support a multilateral diplomatic channel to find some solution. There is no need for more security dilemmas in the region. The US should encourage a political solution. The more US involves itself militarily, it will "justify" China's military buildup (Interview on December 4, 2017). In somewhat a similar expression, Batongbacal said historically, the US has been playing a role of power balancing. The US used to have bases in the Philippines, which tended to promote stability and circumspection. But it lost those bases in 1992 after the US-PHL Military Bases Agreement expired. Since then, the US has tried to maintain its regional presence through special or commercial access arrangements (e.g., Philippines, Singapore). Given China's expansion of its military capabilities, none of the Southeast Asian countries can confront it. Claimant states must take the lead in creating an atmosphere conducive for genuine peaceful settlement. The US should play only a supporting role and support calls for international law to be respected. It is discouraging that the Trump administration is failing to articulate its policies on the Asia Pacific and the SCS (Interview on November 30, 2017).

But for Djalal, outsiders of the SCS should be very careful, otherwise they may be accused of complicating the issue. The US has been very active in the region and it is being accused by China as complicating the issue. Even the big countries in the region such as China can also be accused of bullying the smaller nations. If the role of US is not desired by the countries concerned, it should not interfere. Of course, the US is saying that its policy is about freedom of navigation and overflight. But China maintains that its own policy or actions in the SCS is not affecting freedom of navigation and overflight. While the US is advocating freedom of navigation and overflight, it is placing underwater detecting military devices in the SCS. The irony is that the US is not a party to UNCLOS, and therefore, its position is not a convincing argument (Interview on January 19, 2018). Taking a different approach, Arif said it is not a matter of should or should not. It is rather a matter of will or will not. There will come a time when China crosses the threshold, which will compel or force the US to assert its power in the region. Maybe the US is now playing a more active role in the Asia Pacific than in the last two years, primarily because of the tension in the Korean peninsula. Eventually the US will play a more active role (Interview on January 22, 2018).

Muhibat sees the need for US engagement, though with some differing opinions. For example, Indonesia wants the US to be active in the region through ASEAN, ARF and AMM summits but does not want to see the presence of US military (Interview on December 13, 2017). In somewhat a similar tone, Guan said it all depends on how one views the US. Those who believe in the Cold War paradigm say the role of the US is necessary, but for those who are skeptical of that paradigm, the role of the US is not necessary. It is necessary to look at regional security architecture and the domestic politics of each country. The US is the only country that can balance China in the SCS, but the Trump administration is unpredictable and unreliable (Interview on December 20, 2017). And Lean believes that for ASEAN claimant states, there is a general desire for the US to remain in the region, but the problem is that not all ASEAN states have the same view on the issue as to what the US should do. ASEAN states want other states such as Japan, Australia, Canada, the UK and India to fill the void left by the US. They believe that the US military presence is important for the overall stability of the region. For example, countries such as Vietnam and Singapore are more visible about their view on this but other states are not so, but that does not mean that they do not like the US presence. The ASEAN states see the US as the only country that could contain China; perhaps Cambodia is the exception (Interview on December 26, 2017). Sharing a similar view, Hiep said, most countries in the region prefer to play offshore balancer against China. Since China is big and all other states are small, it will be a great challenge for these small countries to do that. The US should play a more active role. Vietnam has not made an official stance on Trump's offer of mediating the SCS disputes. The proposal is not realistic, but it may be if the claimant states themselves make such a request for the US to play a mediator role. The US should continue what they are doing now. They should provide technological assistance for maritime capacity building and transfer vessels and boats to Vietnam and the Philippines. It should maintain its military presence in the region, such as aircraft carriers. It should also keep its strong navy partnership with regional claimant states in order to maintain a robust military presence (Interview on December 22, 2017).

However, Beckman said the US has its own problems with China and so it cannot be trusted to be a mediator. The US says that China's claims are not consistent with the law of the sea, but the US is not a signatory to UNCLOS (Interview on December 15, 2017). Chaturvedy also questions how much of a role the US can play in the region. It is especially difficult to predict under the Trump administration. Occasional freedom of navigation operation shows that this sea is open and the US can come to the region. There will be more US partners in the region, such as Japan. The US will sell arms to Vietnam. The US is encouraging its international partners or regional institutions such as ASEAN to play a more active role. The US will continue to play a role in the region, but it is difficult to predict how much and for how long. But they will remain, at least for the foreseeable future (Interview on December 21, 2017).

Conclusion

Like many other security issues in global politics, the international community has been divided on the question of the SCS disputes. While some countries support the position of China, some others support the Philippines and other ASEAN claimant states. There are also countries that prefer to remain neutral and support the rule of law, including UNCLOS. Countries such as the US, Australia, Japan, India and others have openly supported the respect for international law and the peaceful resolution of the SCS disputes. Among others, the role of the US has increasingly become more important on the issue. The US, which basically demands freedom of navigation and overflight, is seen as the only naval power that is capable of counterbalancing the increasing assertiveness of China. While the US maintains that it does not support the sovereignty claim of any particular state, it has increasingly become concerned with China rising in the region. This is evident from the US naval forces patrolling the SCS periodically to assert its call for freedom of navigation and overflight in international waters. The US concern is shared by some naval powers of the region which gave rise to the Quad. While the Quad has the potential to bring stability in the region or even balance the rise of China, it still largely remains a dialogue forum than a security alliance.

Conclusions

Prospect of the disputes

The SCS disputes involve both island and maritime claims among sovereign states, and the issue has long been a point of debate in international politics. It involves not only the countries in dispute but also other major powers, including the US. The important strategic location and the largely untapped abundant resources make the SCS a target of contention among the claimant states. The arbitral ruling in July 2016 gave a new momentum to the disputes. The underlying problem is the claim of overlapping areas by different countries, involving China, Brunei, Malaysia, Vietnam, the Philippines, and Taiwan. The disputes between China and Vietnam, and China and the Philippines, have been particularly tense in recent years. There have been numerous works that analyze not only the nature of the disputes or the claims but also prescribe possible solutions. This book is an attempt to contribute to the ongoing debate on the issue and to the existing literature on territorial and maritime disputes.

Theoretical debates and the South China Sea disputes

For realists, the premise of security and order rests on military strength possessed by the state and the alliances formed by the state to ensure balance of power. The inevitable outcome of the absence of any central authority is the phenomenon of forming alliances, groups in order to protect themselves from predators. On the other hand, the liberalists assume that peace can be sustained in the global order with the constant engagement within the republican states, trade exchanges and interdependence under a defined body of law and a sound system of international law. Liberalism also believes that a federation of interdependent states will bring peace and ensure global security. However, constructivists argue that international disputes, such as the SCS is socially constructed, that is, not given by nature and hence, capable of being transformed by human practice. The ASEAN Way of dispute or conflict management tells us how an attempt is made to resolve the SCS dispute through dialogue and peaceful means. The interplay of power politics in the SCS show that elements of all the aforementioned

IR theories and the ASEAN resolution mechanism have some degree of relevance and importance. The competing and/or overlapping claims have made it harder for finding a mutually agreeable plan to pursue or adopt one single strategy toward dispute management and conflict settlement. Given the past instances of confrontation and the imbalance of power between China and the other claimant states, the ASEAN Way of dispute management becomes an important channel of communication, and more importantly for the prevention of military conflict.

The power rivalry between China and the US and its allies show that the realists' perspective of security arrangement or power politics has been on active pursuance. China wants to show, at least its actions suggest, that it is the superpower in the region and its behavior needs to be recognized and respected. At the same time, Beijing is quite conscious that it needs friends and partners in the SCS region and beyond for economic development and sustainability, which is evident from its bilateral ties with countries in the region including the claimant states as well as its broader vision under the BRI initiatives. Though the liberalists would have liked all claimant states to respect international law, such as the UNCLOS, there is enough evidence to suggest that international norms cannot or have not resolved the SCS disputes, at least for now. The constructivists would argue that land reclamations and artificial island buildings, especially by China, have complicated and/or exacerbated the disputes. And the agreement to pursue the disputes through discussion under the COC between China and the other claimant states suggests that the ASEAN Way of dispute management is being pursued as well. But the problem with the COC is the differences over the question of whether the code will eventually be legally binding or not, which China has been reluctant to commit in the past. Even if China eventually agrees to have a legally binding document, as envisaged by the ASEAN states, whether it will actually follow through on all issues related to the SCS disputes, including sovereignty claims, is a lingering doubt. In the event that China decides to renege on its promises, who will then enforce the law or make Beijing accountable? The tribunal ruling in July 2016 was binding under UNCLOS provisions but when China refused to uphold, there was no international mechanism in place to hold China accountable. The ASEAN Way is also complicated by the fact that not all ten ASEAN members are claimants in the SCS. ASEAN littoral states have overlapping claims among themselves. The internal disputes among ASEAN members further complicate the regional bloc's ability to establish a common position. Moreover, because of its economic and military powers, China has been able to influence or coopt some of the ASEAN members.

Theorization

In the introduction, it was hypothesized that claimant states are likely to accept an agreement when the application of international mechanisms serves their individual interest more than the common interests. The research shows that while there is certain truth to the hypothesis, it does not fully explain the entire problem. One important reason why international organizations or institutions fail to deliver a mutually acceptable solution, despite the endorsement by many states, is due to lack of or the absence of enforcement mechanism in the institutions to ensure its effective implementation. In the SCS disputes, China's unparalleled economic and military powers have given it the advantage to ignore or disregard the interests of other claimant states and even to the extent of refusing to oblige the call for multilateralism or to respect international law. The COC, if successfully agreed and implemented, can be a temporary solution for activities such as joint initiatives, exploration, environmental protection, sharing of resources and so forth. But it is unlikely to resolve the sovereignty claims of each claimant state. Then the question is whether China will eventually reach bilateral agreement with all the claimant states, either through persuasion or coercion. Or, will the regional security alliance such as the Quad play an important role on the issue, or at least deter China's increasing assertiveness? Or, will the US decide to intervene more aggressively in the future? These are some inherently important but difficult questions to answer with certainty.

The way forward?

Because of the complicated nature of the problem, finding a solution to the SCS disputes is easier said than done. Apparently, even among leaders from the claimant states and subject experts, there are differing opinions on where the issue is headed. Oegroseno believes that the way forward is to manage the dispute. If claimants are brave enough, they can go to the court for clarity. But maybe they don't have the strength to go to the court. International law is very clear that you need to engage your neighbors peacefully. International law also says that states have international obligations (Interview on January 18, 2018). For Tran, the short-term way forward is the COC between ASEAN and China, how China is willing to negotiate and how other countries are willing to accept the outcome. The US will continue to call on China to stop reclamation activities and militarization of the features until the issue is resolved and international law is respected. The SCS dispute has been there for several decades and the issue has to be resolved by the claimant states (Interview on January 26, 2018).

For Vermonte, the COC completion is the way forward since both China and the ASEAN claimants have made a commitment to the process. All parties need to show restraint in order not to provoke one another, either through statements or actions (Interview on January 29, 2018). Along similar line, Agusman said the way forward is for China to cooperate with ASEAN in the COC process. The COC is not for resolving but to manage the disputes peacefully. No force can resolve the SCS issue since UNCLOS has already clarified the features. By mutual agreement they can go to a third party. Referring to the third party is not easy, especially for China. It is best to maintain the status quo and work on the COC, and wait for a good time to deal with the issue. Maybe the next generation can do that (Interview on January 23, 2018). Sim also shared the view that the COC negotiated by ASEAN and China seems to be the most politically viable way to manage the dispute and to prevent major conflicts in the SCS (Interview on December 18, 2017).

The author's conversation with staff members of the Philippines Foreign Affairs department show that the way forward is to cooperate on the soft areas in order to build confidence, trust and marine environment protection. Claimant states need to cooperate on the non-contentious issues such as search and rescue, safety of navigation, and combating transnational crimes. Later on, they can deal with the hard security issues such as militarization and resources. The Philippines is open to joint exploration, provided that it is under the Philippines' laws, which means China's involvement should be a service contract. In that way, it will be purely a business adventure. Maritime solution should be based on the UNCLOS (Group Discussion on November 28, 2017). But for Musor, the only way forward is to keep on talking and engaging each other at different levels through bilateral and multilateral forums such as the Regional Comprehensive Economic Partnership, being negotiated by ASEAN, which includes other powers. War should be the last resort. Talking should not stop. ASEAN has been criticized for being too slow and having no political teeth. But one should also remember that ASEAN has maintained peace and economic development despite the differences in culture, language, and political ideology. The region has not seen any major military conflict. The fact that they are talking shows that there is a positive development. One should be more worried if the talk is stopped (Interview on December 22, 2017).

While many are optimistic about the possible outcome of the COC, Chua said China and ASEAN are trying to work on the COC, but it will not be very useful. Having a COC will prevent China from taking over the SCS. It is in China's interest to make the COC work because Beijing wants to be seen as cooperative and not disruptive (Interview on December 13, 2017). But for Carpio, the way forward is to follow the law of the sea and share the benefits among all the coastal states, in such a way that all can agree to preserve peace and stability. Except China, all other claimant states stand behind the July 2016 arbitral ruling. The best deal will be for China to share the benefits with other coastal states. Unless China does so, all other claimant states will continue to distrust it. People will never allow their governments to give up their sovereignty claims (Interview on December 8, 2017).

And for Lean, the most popular solution will be joint development of resources, mainly oil and gas. But the question is, if you ask the Philippines and Vietnam, will they agree to China's proposal. If they agree, do they concede to China's claims? The question of who will ensure equitable benefit of the parties requires a lot of negotiation and compromise. The way forward is not very optimistic. It is a roller coaster ride with ups and downs. This cycle will continue. No government in the region can give a solution to the entire SCS disputes. The future is very precarious. If China is willing to compromise on their claims, maybe there can be a possibility one day. Whether the COC will be successful or not will depend on China's attitude because it wants to decide everything. China knows that it is a key player and wants to continue that way (Interview on December 26, 2017).

Unsurprisingly, there are differing views not only about the fundamental issues of the SCS disputes but also on how to move forward. Then the question is whether the claimants will eventually be willing to abandon their confrontational attitude and agree to find some common ground, even if it requires sacrificing certain portions of their claims. For example, one possible peaceful solution would be for all claimants to limit their claim to the areas of 200 nautical miles of the EEZ and continental shelf in accordance with the UNCLOS. By agreeing to such proposal, the parties to the dispute can also reach an agreement to leave international waters for free navigation and overflight. But the July 2016 arbitration and the Chinese refusal have indicated that the existing international law is unable, or at least unlikely, to address the SCS disputes in the near future.

Another possibility may be for the parties concerned to establish a common ownership of the disputed areas whereby all the revenues from the SCS are equitably or proportionately shared among the littoral states. But this can also be a problem because of the varying levels of claims made by the coastal states. For example, who will decide who gets what and how much. It is a challenge whether the claimant states can reach an agreement on resource and/or benefit sharing. As the US is a non-claimant state, theoretically it is in a position to highlight violations committed by individual claimants in international forums, such as the UN Security Council. But because of the great power rivalry between China and the US, Washington's neutrality on the issue is questionable. Moreover, since the US is not a party to the UNCLOS, its voice on the compliance of law of the sea is not taken seriously by many. On the other hand, because of China's unparalleled military power in the region, the US navy is the only reliable guarantor of freedom of navigation. Other claimants will be outpowered in the event of any future violation of treaty(s) by China. The disunity among ASEAN members on the issue also means that the claimant states either reach bilateral agreement with China or seek the support of the US and other like-minded members of the international community, such as Australia, Japan and India, to protect and safeguard their interests. A security alliance like the Quad may be another possible way to collectively restrain or contain or check the increasing assertiveness of China, but up to now the pact appears to be a mere dialogue forum.

Peace could perhaps prevail in the SCS when the claimants choose stability of the region rather than the potential benefits they each individually intend to yield; when the claimants give priority to domestic and international developmental projects over their competing demands; when the claimants respect and accept the application and implementation of relevant international laws as opposed to their individual interests; when the claimants are prepared to compromise and sacrifice their respective claims and instead focus on improving their bilateral economic and political ties other than the SCS; and when the claimants agree to share the resources of the waters and allow the freedom of navigation and overflight. While there are possible areas of cooperation or even a potential solution to the protracted conflict, there are also several challenges and difficulties. Until an amicable solution is achieved, all possible options should be explored and pursued, including the COC and bilateral dialogue among the claimant states, while restraining from actions that could escalate tensions or jeopardize existing dialogue mechanisms. China also needs to respect relevant international laws as a responsible member of the international community, particularly being a signatory to the UNCLOS. Ultimately, given the nature and level of complexity, a peaceful solution to the SCS disputes will require compromises and sacrifices from all claimant states, as well as the support and cooperation of other regional and international naval powers which have direct or indirect interest in the issue.

Figure 6.1 Author with Antonio T. Carpio (senior associate justice of the Supreme Court, Supreme Court of the Philippines) at his office on December 8, 2017

Source: Author.

Figure 6.2 Author with Professor Robert Beckman (head, Ocean Law and Policy Programme, Centre for International Law, National University of Singapore) at his office on December 15, 2017

Source: Author.

Figure 6.3 Author with Arif Havas Oegroseno (deputy coordinating minister for maritime sovereignty, Coordinating Ministry for Maritime Affairs, Government of the Republic of Indonesia) at his office in Jakarta on January 18, 2018

Source: Author.

Figure 6.4 Author with Aileen Baviera (professor, Department of Political Science, University of the Philippines) at her office on December 4, 2017

Source: Author.

Figure 6.5 Author with Le Hong Hiep (fellow, ISEAS-Yusof Ishak Institute, National University of Singapore) on December 22, 2017

Source: Author.

Bibliography

Reports

Cronin, Patrick M. 2014. *The Challenge of Responding to Maritime Coercion.* Washington, DC: Center for a New American Security.

Fravel, M. Taylor. 2014. "Policy Report: U.S. Policy Towards the Disputes in the South China Sea Since 1995." *S. Rajaratnam School of International Studies*, March, 1–10.

Glaser, Bonnie S. 2014. "U.S. Strategy Seeks to Calm the Roiled Waters of the South China Sea." In *Perspectives on the South China Sea: Diplomatic, Legal, and Security Dimensions of the Dispute*, edited by Murray Hiebert, Phuong Nguyen and Gregory B. Poling, 53–62. Washington, DC: Center for Strategic & International Studies.

Hiebert, Murray, Phuong Nguyen and Gregory B. Poling. 2014. *Perspectives on the South China Sea: Diplomatic, Legal, and Security Dimensions of the Dispute.* Washington, DC: Center for Strategic & International Studies.

Koda, Yoji. 2014. "Japan's Perspectives on U.S. Policy Toward the South China Sea." In *Perspectives on the South China Sea: Diplomatic, Legal, and Security Dimensions of the Dispute*, edited by Murray Hiebert, Phuong Nguyen and Gregory B. Poling, 82–95. Washington, DC: Center for Strategic & International Studies.

Parameswaran, Prashanth. 2015. "Playing It Safe: Malaysia's Approach to the South China Sea and Implications for the United States." *Center for a New American Security*, February, 1–14.

Rapp-Hooper, Mira and Harry Krejsa. 2016. *Reefs, Rocks, and the Rule of Law: After the Arbitration in the South China Sea.* Washington, DC: Center for a New American Security.

Roach, J. Ashley. 2014. "Malaysia and Brunei: An Analysis of Their Claims in the South China Sea." *A CNA Occasional Paper*, August, 1–43.

Rosen, Mark E. 2014. "Philippine Claims in the South China Sea: A Legal Analysis." *A CAN Occasional Paper*, August, 1–49.

Interviews/group discussions

Agusman, Damos Dumoli (Director General for International Law & Treaties, Ministry of Foreign Affairs). Semi-Structured Interview. Jakarta, January 23, 2018.

Almuttaqi, A. Ibrahim (Head of ASEAN Studies Program, The Habibie Center). Semi-Structured Interview. Jakarta, January 22, 2018.

Amador, Julio (Former Deputy Director General, Foreign Service Institute, and Advisor to ASEAN Studies Center, New Era University). Semi-Structured Interview. Quezon, December 7, 2017.

Ariadno, Melda Kamil (Professor, Faculty of Law, University of Indonesia). Semi-Structured Interview. Depok, January 25, 2018.

Arif, Muhamad (Researcher, ASEAN Studies Program, The Habibie Center). Semi-Structured Interview. Jakarta, January 22, 2018.

Banlaoi, Rommel (Vice President of Philippine Association for Chinese Studies (PACS) and Professorial Lecturer, Department of International Studies, College of Arts and Sciences, Miriam College). Semi-Structured Interview. Quezon, December 5, 2017.

Bata, Sidney Christopher T. (Lecturer, Chinese Studies Program, Ateneo de Manila University). Semi-Structured Interview. Quezon, November 29, 2017.

Batongbacal, Jay (Associate Professor, College of Law, University of the Philippines, and Director, Institute for Maritime Affairs & Law of the Sea). Semi-Structured Interview. Quezon, November 30, 2017.

Baviera, Aileen (Professor, Department of Political Science, University of the Philippines). Semi-Structured Interview. Quezon, December 4, 2017.

Beckman, Robert (Head, Ocean Law and Policy Programme, Centre for International Law, National University of Singapore). Semi-Structured Interview. Singapore, December 15, 2017.

Carpio, Antonio T. (Senior Associate Justice of the Supreme Court, Supreme Court of the Philippines). Semi-Structured Interview. Manila, December 8, 2017.

Chalermpalanupap, Termsak (Fellow, ISEAS-Yusof Ishak Institute, National University of Singapore). Semi-Structured Interview. Singapore, December 22, 2017.

Chaturvedy, Rajeev Ranjan (Research Associate, Institute of South Asian Studies, National University of Singapore). Semi-Structured Interview. Singapore, December 21, 2017.

Chua, Daniel (Assistant Professor and Deputy Head of Graduate Studies, S. Rajaratnam School of International Studies, Nanyang Technological University). Semi-Structured Interview. Singapore, December 13, 2017.

Chye, Tan Seng (Senior Fellow, S. Rajaratnam School of International Studies, Nanyang Technological University). Semi-Structured Interview. Singapore, December 18, 2017.

Djalal, Hasjim (Member of Indonesian Maritime Council, Senior Advisor to the Indonesian Minister for Maritime Affairs and Fisheries, and to Indonesian Naval Chief of Staff; Former Indonesian Ambassador to Germany, Canada, and the United Nations). Semi-Structured Interview. Jakarta, January 19, 2018.

Encomienda, Alberto (Executive Director of balikBalangay Inc., Former Secretary-General of the (then) Maritime and Ocean Affairs Center, Department of Foreign Affairs and Philippines' Former Ambassador to Greece, Malaysia and Singapore). Semi-Structured Interview. Manila, December 1, 2017.

Guan, Kwa Chong (Senior Fellow, S. Rajaratnam School of International Studies, Nanyang Technological University). Semi-Structured Interview. Singapore, December 20, 2017.

Gungwu, Wang (Chairman, East Asian Institute and Professor, National University of Singapore). Semi-Structured Interview. Singapore, December 19, 2017.

Hiep, Le Hong (Fellow, ISEAS-Yusof Ishak Institute, National University of Singapore). Semi-Structured Interview. Singapore, December 22, 2017.

Hikmahanto, Juwana (Professor, Faculty of Law, University of Indonesia). Semi-Structured Interview. Jakarta, January 18, 2018.

Hongzhou, Zhang (Research Fellow, S. Rajaratnam School of International Studies, Nanyang Technological University). Semi-Structured Interview. Singapore, December 20, 2017.

Joaquin, Rhodora (Supervising Foreign Affairs Research Specialist), Fides Quintos (Senior Foreign Affairs Research Specialist), and Jeremy Dexter B. Mirasol (Foreign Affairs Research Specialist I), Center for International Relations and Strategic Studies, Foreign Service Institute, Department of Foreign Affairs). Group Discussion. Pasay, November 28, 2017.

Kembara, Gilang (Researcher, International Relations Department, Centre for Strategic and International Studies). Semi-Structured Interview. Jakarta, January 18, 2018.

Kraft, Herman Joseph (Associate Professor, Department of Political Science, University of the Philippines). Semi-Structured Interview. Quezon, November 29, 2017.

Krisman, Khanisa (Researcher on ASEAN and Southeast Asian Issue), Sri Nuryanti (Head of Research Management and Dissemination), and Awani Irewati MA (Chief of International Research Groups), Centre for Political Studies, Indonesian Institute of Sciences). Group Discussion. Jakarta, January 26, 2018.

Lean, Collin Koh Swee (Research Fellow, Maritime Security Programme, S. Rajaratnam School of International Studies Offices, Nanyang Technological University). Semi-Structured Interview. Singapore, December 26, 2017.

Muhibat, Shafiah Fifi (Senior Fellow, Maritime Security Programme, S. Rajaratnam School of International Studies, Nanyang Technological University). Semi-Structured Interview. Singapore, December 13, 2017.

Musor, Gonaranao B. (First Secretary and Consul and Head of the Political, Economic and Cultural Sections, Embassy of the Philippines, Singapore). Semi-Structured Interview. Singapore, December 22, 2017.

Nan, Li (Senior Research Fellow, East Asian Institute, National University of Singapore). Semi-Structured Interview. Singapore, December 19, 2017.

Naval, Jaime B. (Assistant Professor, Department of Political Science, University of the Philippines). Semi-Structured Interview. Quezon, December 6, 2017.

Nugroho, Haryo Budi (Law of the Sea Expert, Office of the Special Envoy to the President of Indonesia for Maritime Delimitation). Semi-Structured Interview. Jakarta, January 24, 2018.

Oegroseno, Arif Havas (Deputy Coordinating Minister for Maritime Sovereignty – Coordinating Ministry for Maritime Affairs, also Former Director General for Legal Affairs and Treaties, President of the 20th Session of the State Parties Meeting of United Nations Convention on the Law of the Sea). Semi-Structured Interview. Jakarta, January 18, 2018.

Papa, Alcuin (Managing Editor of ANC (ABS-CBN)). Semi-Structured Interview. Quezon, December 7, 2017.

Pattiradjawane, Rene L. (Senior Journalist and Chair of the Foundation for the Centre for Chinese Studies). Semi-Structured Interview. Jakarta, January 17, 2018.

Sim, Christine (Research Associate and Practice Fellow, Centre for International Law, National University of Singapore). Semi-Structured Interview. Singapore, December 18, 2017.

Siregar, Tjoki Aprianda (Minister Counsellor, Embassy of the Republic of Indonesia, Singapore). Semi-Structured Interview. Singapore, December 20, 2017.

Tavares, Jose Antonio Morato (Director General for ASEAN Cooperation and Former Indonesian Ambassador to New Zealand, Samoa and the Kingdom of Tonga). Semi-Structured Interview. Jakarta, January 20, 2018.

Tello, Rafael De Bustamante (First Counsellor and Head of Political, Press and Information Section, European Union, Delegation of the European Union to Indonesia and Brunei Darussalam). Semi-Structured Interview. Jakarta, January 16, 2018.

Tran, Teresa (Political Officer, US Embassy Jakarta). Semi-Structured Interview. Jakarta, January 26, 2018.

Tseng, Katherine Hui-Yi (Research Associate, East Asian Institute, National University of Singapore). Semi-Structured Interview. Singapore, December 19, 2017.

Vermonte, Philips J. (Executive Director, Centre for Strategic and International Studies). Semi-Structured Interview. Jakarta, January 29, 2018.

Wisnu, Dinna (Associate Professor, Department of International Relations & Diplomacy of Bina Nusantara University Jakarta, Co-founder of Paramadina Graduate School of Diplomacy & Indonesia's Representative to the ASEAN Intergovernmental Commission on Human Rights 2016–2018). Semi-Structured Interview. Jakarta, January 22, 2018.

Xue, Gong (Research Fellow, China Programme, Rajaratnam School of International Studies, Nanyang Technological University). Semi-Structured Interview. Singapore, December 12, 2017.

Books and journals

Agnew, John. 2015. "The Geopolitics of Knowledge About World Politics: A Case Study in U.S. Hegemony." In *Geographies of Knowledge and Power*, edited by P. Meusburger, D. Gregory and L. Suarsana, 235–246. London: Springer.

Agnew, John. 2010. "Emerging China and Critical Geopolitics: Between World Politics and Chinese Particularity." *Eurasian Geography and Economics* 51(5): 569–582.

Amer, Ramses. 1999. "Conflict Management and Constructive Engagement in ASEAN's Expansion." *Third World Quarterly* 20(5): 1031–1048.

Aoyama, Rumi. 2016. " 'One Belt, One Road': China's New Global Strategy." *Journal of Contemporary East Asia Studies* 5(2): 3–22.

Aust, Anthony. 2010. *Handbook of International Law*. New York: Cambridge University Press.

Barkin, J. Samuel. 2010. *Realist Constructivism: Rethinking International Relations Theory*. Cambridge: Cambridge University Press.

Bateman, Sam. 2011. "Regime Building in the South China Sea – Current Situation and Outlook." *Australian Journal of Maritime & Ocean Affairs* 3(1): 25–33.

Bautista, Lowell. 2014. "The Arbitration Case Between Philippines and China Over Their Dispute in the South China Sea." *Jati* 19: 3–24.

Baviera, Aileen S. P. 2016. "China's Strategic Foreign Initiatives Under Xi Jinping: An ASEAN Perspective." *China Quarterly of International Strategic Studies* 2(1): 57–79.

Beeson, Mark and Fujian Li. 2015. "What Consensus? Geopolitics and Policy Paradigms in China and the United States." *International Affairs* 91(1): 93–109.

Blackwill, Robert and Ashley Tellis. 2015. *Revising US Grand Strategy Towards China*. New York: Council on Foreign Relations.

Blussé, Leonard. 1999. "Chinese Century: The Eighteenth Century in the China Sea Region." *Archipel* 58: 107–129.

Blussé, Leonard. 1996. "No Boats to China. The Dutch East India Company and the Changing Pattern of the China Sea Trade, 1635–1690." *Modern Asian Studies* 30(1): 51–76.

Breslin, Shaun. 2010. "China's Emerging Global Role: Dissatisfied Responsible Great Power." *Politics* 30(1): 52–62.

Brunnée, Jutta and Stephen J. Toope. 2013. "Constructivism and International Law." In *Interdisciplinary Perspectives on International Law and International Relations: The State of the Art*, edited by Jeffrey L. Dunoff and Mark A. Pollack, 119–145. Cambridge: Cambridge University Press.

Buss, David M. 1995. "Evolutionary Psychology: A New Paradigm for Psychological Science." *Psychological Inquiry* 6(1): 1–30.

Buszynski, Leszek. 2012. "The South China Sea: Oil, Maritime Claims, and U.S.-China Strategic Rivalry." *The Washington Quarterly* 35(2): 139–156.

Buszynski, Leszek and Iskandar Sazlan. 2007. "Maritime Claims and Energy Cooperation in the South China Sea." *Contemporary Southeast Asia* 29(1): 143–171.

Caballero-Anthony, Mely. 1998. "Mechanisms of Dispute Settlement: The ASEAN Experience." *Contemporary Southeast Asia* 20(1): 38–66.

Callahan, William. 2015. "History, Tradition and the China Dream: Socialist Modernization in the World of Great Harmony." *Journal of Contemporary China* 24(96): 983–1001.

Callahan, William. 2009. "The Cartography of National Humiliation and the Emergence of China's Geobody." *Public Culture* 21(1): 141–173.

Calvo, Alex. 2015. "China, the Philippines, Vietnam, and International Arbitration in the South China Sea." *The Asia-Pacific Journal* 13(43, 2): 1–54.

Chai, Winberg. 1999. "Relations Between the Chinese Mainland and Taiwan: Overview and Chronology." *Asian Affairs* 26(2): 59–76.

Chemillier-Gendreau, Monique. 2000. *Sovereignty Over the Paracel and Spratly Islands*. The Hague: Kluwer Law International.

Chen, Hurng-yu. 2014. "Territorial Disputes in the South China Sea Under the San Francisco Peace Treaty." *Issues and Studies* 50(3): 169–196.

Chen, Hurng-yu. 1993. "A Comparison Between Taipei and Peking in Their Policies and Concepts Regarding South China Sea." *Issues and Studies* 29(9): 22–55.

Chen, Tian Shi. 1928. *Compilation of Files of the Paracel and Pratas Islands, Files of the Paracel Islands*. Shanghai: The Commercial Press Ltd.

Chiu, Hungdah and Choon-Ho Park. 1975. "Legal Status of the Paracel and Spratly Islands." *Ocean Development and International Law Journal* 3(1): 1–28.

Choi, Jong Kun and Yong-Soo Eun. 2018. "What Does International Relations Theory Tell Us About Territorial Disputes and Their Resolution?" *International Politics* 55(2): 141–159.

Chung, Chris P. C. 2016. "Drawing the U-Shaped Line: China's Claim in the South China Sea, 1946–1974." *Modern China* 42(1): 38–72.

Churchill, Robin Rolf and Alan Vaughan Lowe. 1999. *The Law of the Sea*. Manchester: Manchester University Press.

Coulter, Daniel Yarrow. 1996. "South China Sea Fisheries: Countdown to Calamity." *Contemporary Southeast Asia* 17(4): 371–388.

Cox, Robert W. 1981. "Social Forces, States and World Orders: Beyond International Relations Theory." *Millennium: Journal of International Studies* 10(2): 126–155.

Cronin, Bruce. 2001. "The Paradox of Hegemony: America's Ambiguous Relationship with the United Nations." *European Journal of International Relations* 7(1): 103–130.

Cronin, Patrick M. and Robert D. Kaplan. 2012. "Cooperation from Strength: U.S. Strategy and the South China Sea." In *Cooperation from Strength: The United States, China and the South China Sea*, edited by Patrick M. Cronin, 3–30. Washington, DC: Center for a New American Security.

Dang, Vu Hai. 2014. "Disputes Between Vietnam and China in the South China Sea: A Legal Analysis." In *Perspectives on the South China Sea Diplomatic, Legal, and Security Dimensions of the Dispute*, edited by Murray Hiebert, Phuong Nguyen and Gregory B. Poling, 35–44. Washington, DC: Center for Strategic & International Studies.

Djalal, Hasjim. 2001. "Indonesia and the South China Sea Initiative." *Ocean Development and International Law* 32(2): 97–105.

Djalal, Hasjim. 2000. "South China Sea Island Disputes." *The Raffles Bulletin of Zoology* 8: 9–21.

Doyle, Michael W. 1997. *Ways of War and Peace: Realism, Liberalism and Socialism*. New York: W. W. Norton & Co Inc.

Duara, Prasenjit. 1995. *Rescuing History from the Nation: Questioning Narratives of Modern China*. London: University of Chicago Press.

Dupuy, Florian and Pierre-Marie Dupuy. 2013. "A Legal Analysis of China's Historic Rights Claim in the South China Sea." *The American Journal of International Law* 107(1): 124–141.

Dutton, Peter. 2011. "Three Disputes and Three Objectives: China and the South China Sea." *Naval War College Review* 64(4): 42–67.

Dzurek, Daniel J. 1996. *The Spratly Islands Dispute: Who's on First?* Durham: International Boundaries Research Unit, University of Durham.

Etzioni, Amitai. 2016. "Freedom of Navigation Assertions: The United States as the World's Policeman." *Armed Forces & Society* 42(3): 501–517.

Fierke, Karin M. 2013. "Constructivism." In *International Relations Theories: Discipline and Diversity*, edited by Tim Dunne, Milja Kurki and Steve Smith, 187–204. Oxford: Oxford University Press.

Fravel, Mark T. 2014. "Territorial and Maritime Boundary Disputes in Asia." In *Oxford Handbook of the International Relations of Asia*, edited by S. Pekkanen, J. Ravenhill and R. Foot, 524–546. Oxford: Oxford University Press.

Fravel, Mark T. 2011. "China's Strategy in the South China Sea." *Contemporary Southeast Asia* 33(3): 292–319.

Fravel, Mark T. 2005. "Regime Insecurity and International Cooperation: Explaining China's Compromises in Territorial Disputes." *International Security* 30(2): 46–83.

Friedberg, Aaron L. 2014. "The Sources of Chinese Conduct: Explaining Beijing's Assertiveness." *The Washington Quarterly* 37(4): 133–150.

Friedberg, Aaron L. 2011. *A Contest for Supremacy: China, America, and the Struggle for Mastery in Asia*. New York: W. W. Norton & Co Inc.

Gallagher, Michael G. 1994. "China's Illusory Threat to the South China Sea." *International Security* 19(1): 169–194.

Gao, Zhiguo and Bing Bing Jia. 2013. "The Nine-Dash Line in the South China Sea: History, Status, and Implications." *The American Journal of International Law* 107(1): 98–124.

Garver, John W. 1992. "China's Push Through the South China Sea: The Interaction of Bureaucratic and National Interests." *The China Quarterly* 132: 999–1028.

Goldsmith, Jack and Eric Posner. 2005. *The Limits of International Law*. Oxford: Oxford University Press.

Goldstein, Lyle. 2011. "Chinese Naval Strategy in the South China Sea: An Abundance of Noise and Smoke, but Little Fire." *Contemporary Southeast Asia* 33(3): 320–347.

Gonzalez-Vicente, Reuben. 2015. "The Limits to China's Non-interference Foreign Policy: Pro-state Interventionism and the Rescaling of Economic Governance." *Australian Journal of International Affairs* 69(2): 205–223.

Gowan, Peter. 2010. *A Calculus of Power: Grand Strategy in the Twenty-first Century*. London: Verso.

Granados, Ulises. 2008. "Japanese Expansion into the South China Sea: Colonization and Conflict, 1902–1939." *Journal of Asian History* 2(2): 117–142.

Granados, Ulises. 2006. "Chinese Ocean Policies Towards the South China Sea in a Transitional Period, 1946–1952." *The China Review* 6(1): 153–181.

Granados, Ulises. 2005. "As China Meets the Southern Sea Frontier: Ocean Identity in the Making, 1902–1937." *Pacific Affairs* 78(3): 443–461.

Guan, Ang Cheng. 2000. "The South China Sea Dispute Revisited." *Australian Journal of International Affairs* 54(2): 201–215.

Gungwu, Wang. 1998. *The Nanhai Trade: The Early History of Chinese Trade in the South China Sea*. Singapore: Times Academic Press.

Gupta, Sonika. 2005. "Chinese Strategies for Resolution of the Taiwan and South China Sea Disputes." *International Studies* 42(3–4): 247–264.

Guzman, Andrew T. 2008. *How International Law Works: A Rational Choice Theory*. Oxford: Oxford University Press.

Hameiri, Shahar and Lee Jones. 2016. "Rising Powers and State Transformation: The Case of China." *European Journal of International Relations* 22(1): 72–98.

Hayton, Bill. 2018. "The Modern Creation of China's 'Historic Rights' Claim in the South China Sea." *Asian Affairs* 49(3): 370–382.

Hayton, Bill. 2014. *The South China Sea: The Struggle for Power in Asia*. New Haven and London: Yale University Press.

Heydarian, Richard Javad. 2017. "Duterte's Geopolitical Game-play." In *Line in the Waters: The South China Sea Dispute and Its Implications for Asia*, edited by Abhijit Singh, 55–63. New Delhi: Observer Research Foundation.

Hiep, Le Hong. 2013. "Vietnam's Hedging Strategy Against China Since Normalization." *Contemporary Southeast Asia* 35(3): 333–368.

Hindley, Michael and James Bridge. 1994. "South China Sea: The Spratly and Paracel Islands Dispute." *The World Today* 50(6): 109–112.

Hong, Zhao. 2016. "China's One Belt One Road: An Overview of the Debate." *ISEAS – Yusof Ishak Institute* 6: 1–33.

Hong, Zhao. 2007. "India and China: Rivals or Partners in Southeast Asia?" *Contemporary Southeast Asia* 29(1): 121–142.

Hopf, Ted. 1998. "The Promise of Constructivism in International Relations Theory." *International Security* 23(1): 171–200.

Hsiao, Anne Hsiu-an and Cheng-yi Lin. 2016. "Taiwan's Evolving Policy Towards the South China Sea Dispute, 1992–2016." In *The South China Sea Dispute: Navigating Diplomatic and Strategic Tensions*, edited by Ian Storey and Cheng-yi Lin, 74–103. Singapore: ISEAS Publishing.

Hsieh, Pasha L. 2009. "The Taiwan Question and the One-China Policy: Legal Challenges with Renewed Momentum." *Die Friedens-Warte* 84(3): 59–81.

Jawli, Nandini. 2016. "South China Sea and India's Geopolitical Interests." *Indian Journal of Asian Affairs* 29(1/2): 85–100.

Jennings, Robert Yewdall. 1963. *The Acquisition of Territory in International Law*. Manchester: Manchester University Press.

Jervis, Robert. 1999. "Realism, Neoliberalism, and Cooperation: Understanding the Debate." *International Security* 24(1): 42–63.

Jilan, Su. 2004. "Overview of the South China Sea Circulation and Its Influence on the Coastal Physical Oceanography Outside the Pearl River Estuary." *Continental Shelf Research* 24: 1745–1760.

Kant, Immanuel. 1970. "Perpetual Peace: A Philosophical Sketch." In *Kant's Political Writings*, edited by Hans Reiss, 93–115. Cambridge: Cambridge University Press.

Kaplan, Robert. 2014. *Asia's Cauldron. The South China Sea and the End of a Stable Pacific*. New York: Random House.

Keohane, Robert O. 2012. "Twenty Years of Institutional Liberalism." *International Relations* 26(2): 125–138.

Keohane, Robert O. 1980. "The Theory of Hegemonic Stability and Changes in International Economic Regimes." In *Change in the International System*, edited by Ole R. Holsti, Randolph M. Siverson and Alexander L. George, 131–162. Boulder, CO: Westview Press.

Keyuan, Zou. 2001. "Historic Rights in International Law and in China's Practice." *Ocean Development & International Law* 32(2): 149–168.

Khong, Yuen Foong. 2013. "Primacy or World Order? The United States and China's Rise – A Review Essay." *International Security* 38(3): 153–175.

Kihl, Young Whan. 1989. "Intra-Regional Conflict and the ASEAN Peace Process." *International Journal* 44(3): 598–615.

Kim, Jihyun. 2015. "Territorial Disputes in the South China Sea Implications for Security in Asia and Beyond." *Strategic Studies Quarterly* 9(2): 107–141.

Kingdon, Emma. 2015. "A Case for Arbitration: The Philippines' Solution for the South China Sea Dispute." *Boston College International and Comparative Law Review* 38(1): 129–157.

Kipgen, Nehginpao. 2018. "ASEAN and China in the South China Sea Disputes." *Asian Affairs* 49(3): 433–448.

Kipgen, Nehginpao. 2016a. *Democratization of Myanmar*. New Delhi: Routledge.

Kipgen, Nehginpao. 2016b. *Myanmar: A Political History*. New Delhi: Oxford University Press.

Kipgen, Nehginpao. 2015. *Democracy Movement in Myanmar: Problems and Challenges*. New Delhi: Ruby Press & Co.

Kirshner, J. 2012. "The Tragedy of Offensive Realism: Classical Realism and the Rise of China." *European Journal of International Relations* 18(1): 53–75.

Kittichaisaree, Kriangsak. 2001. "A Code of Conduct for Human and Regional Security Around the South China Sea." *Ocean Development & International Law* 32(2): 131–148.

Korkut, Ekrem and Woo Hyun Kang. 2017. "China's Nine Dash Line Claim in Light of the Ruling by the Permanent Court of Arbitration (12 July 2016)." *Penn State Journal of Law & International Affairs* 5(2): 426–463.

Ku, Samuel C. Y. 2017. "Strategies of China's Expansion and Taiwan's Survival in Southeast Asia: A Comparative Perspective." In *Taiwan and China: Fitful*

Embrace, edited by Lowell Dittmer, 249–279. Berkeley, CA: University of California Press.

Lebow, Richard Ned. 2013. "Classical Realism." In *International Relations Theories: Discipline and Diversity*, edited by Tim Dunne, Milja Kurki and Steve Smith, 59–76. Oxford: Oxford University Press.

Lee, John. 2013. "Australia's 2015 Defence White Paper: Seeking Strategic Opportunities in Southeast Asia to Help Manage China's Peaceful Rise." *Contemporary Southeast Asia* 35(3): 395–422.

Lee, John. 2011. "Malaysia 'Punching Above Its Weight . . . and Finally Hitting the Target'." *Southeast Asian Affairs* 158–170.

Leifer, Michael. 2001. "Taiwan and South-East Asia: The Limits to Pragmatic Diplomacy." *The China Quarterly* 165: 173–185.

Levathes, Louise. 1994. *When China Ruled the Seas: The Treasure Fleet of the Dragon Throne, 1405–1433*. New York: Simon & Schuster.

Leviter, Lee. 2010. "The ASEAN Charter: ASEAN Failure or Member Failure?" *New York University Journal of International Law and Politics* 43(159): 160–210.

Lin, Cheng-yi. 1997. "Taiwan's South China Sea Policy." *Asian Survey* 37(4): 323–339.

Lingjie, Kong. 2015. "The Belt and Road Initiative and China's Foreign Policy Toward Its Territorial and Boundary Disputes." *China Quarterly of International Strategic Studies* 1(2): 325–345.

Liow, Joseph Chin Yong. 2000. "Malaysia-China Relations in the 1990s: The Maturing of a Partnership." *Asian Survey* 40(4): 672–691.

Lo, Chi-kin. 1989. *China's Policy Towards Territorial Disputes: The Case of the South China Sea Islands*. London and New York: Routledge.

Luttwak, Edward. 2012. *The Rise of China vs. the Logic of Strategy*. Cambridge, MA: Belknap Press.

Malik, Mohan. 2013. "Historical Fiction: China's South China Sea Claims." *World Affairs* 176(1): 83–90.

Marston, Geoffrey. 1986. "Abandonment of Territorial Claims: The Cases of Bouvet and Spratly Islands." *The British Yearbook of International Law* 57(1): 337–356.

McDonald, Matt. 2008. "Constructivism." In *Security Studies: An Introduction*, edited by Paul D. Williams, 59–72. London and New York: Routledge.

Mearsheimer, John J. 2006. "China's Unpeaceful Rise." *Current History* 105(690): 160–162.

Mearsheimer, John J. 1994. "The False Promise of International Institutions." *International Security* 19(3): 5–49.

Minzner, Carl. 2015. "China After the Reform Era." *Journal of Democracy* 26(3): 129–143.

Mohan, C. Raja. 2008. "India's Geopolitics and Southeast Asian Security." *Southeast Asian Affairs* 43–60.

Moravcsik, Andrew. 1995. "Explaining International Human Rights Regimes: Liberal Theory and Western Europe." *European Journal of International Relations* 1(2): 157–189.

Morgenthau, Hans J. 1948. *Politics Among Nations: The Struggle for Power and Peace*. New York: Alfred A. Knopf.

Mowle, Thomas S. 2003. "Worldviews in Foreign Policy: Realism, Liberalism, and External Conflict." *Political Psychology* 24(3): 561–592.

Murfett, Malcolm H., John N. Miksic, Brian P. Farrell and Chiang Ming Shun. 1999. *Between Two Oceans: A Military History of Singapore from the First Settlement to Final British Withdrawal.* Singapore: Oxford University Press.

Narine, Shaun. 1998. "ASEAN and the Management of Regional Security." *Pacific Affairs* 71(2): 195–214.

Narine, Shaun. 1997. "ASEAN and the ARF: The Limits of the 'ASEAN Way'." *Asian Survey* 37(10): 961–978.

Navari, Cornelia. 2008. "Liberalism." In *Security Studies: An Introduction*, edited by Paul D. Williams, 29–43. London and New York: Routledge.

Nishikawa, Yukiko. 2007. "The 'ASEAN Way' and Asian Regional Security." *Politics & Policy* 35(1): 42–56.

Nolan, Peter. 2013. "Imperial Archipelagos: China, Western Colonialism and the Law of the Sea." *New Left Review* 80: 77–95.

Noor, Elina. 2017. "The South China Sea Dispute: Options for Malaysia." In *The South China Sea Dispute: Navigating Diplomatic and Strategic Tensions*, edited by Ian Storey and Cheng-yi Lin, 205–227. New Delhi: Pentagon Press.

Palan, Ronen. 2000. "A World of Their Making: An Evaluation of the Constructivist Critique in International Relations." *Review of International Studies* 26(4): 575–598.

Pan, Chengxin. 2010. "Westphalia and the Taiwan Conundrum: A Case Against the Exclusionist Construction of Sovereignty and Identity." *Journal of Chinese Political Science* 15(4): 371–389.

Pao-min, Chang. 1990. "A New Scramble for the South China Sea Islands." *Contemporary Southeast Asia* 12(1): 20–39.

Papayoanou, Paul A. 1996. "Interdependence, Institutions, and the Balance of Power: Britain, Germany, and World War I." *International Security* 20(4): 42–76.

Pickering, Jeffrey. 1998. *Britain's Withdrawal from East of Suez. The Politics of Retrenchment.* London: Palgrave Macmillan.

Pitcher, Tony J., Reg Watson, Nigel Haggan, Sylvie Guénette, Robin Kennish, Ussif R. Sumaila, David Cook, Keith Wilson and Albert Leung. 2000. "Marine Reserves and the Restoration of Fisheries and Marine Ecosystems in the South China Sea." *Bulletin of Marine Science* 66(3): 543–566.

Posner, Eric A. and John C. Yoo. 2005. "Judicial Independence in International Tribunals." *California Law Review* 93(1): 1–74.

Puri, Raman and Arun Sahgal. 2011. "The South China Sea Dispute: Implications for India." *Indian Foreign Affairs Journal* 6(4): 437–448.

Reis, Filipe dos and Oliver Kessler. 2016. "Constructivism and the Politics of International Law." In *The Oxford Handbook of the Theory of International Law*, edited by Anne Orford and Florian Hoffmann, 344–364. Oxford: Oxford University Press.

Roberts, Christopher. 2011. "BRUNEI DARUSSALAM: Consolidating the Foundations of Its Future?" *Southeast Asian Affairs* 35–50.

Rolf, Steve and John Agnew. 2016. "Sovereignty Regimes in the South China Sea: Assessing Contemporary Sino-US Relations." *Eurasian Geography and Economics* 57(2): 249–273.

Rose, Gideon. 1998. "Review: Neoclassical Realism and Theories of Foreign Policy." *World Politics* 51(1): 144–172.

Rowan, Joshua P. 2005. "The U.S.-Japan Security Alliance, ASEAN, and the South China Sea Dispute." *Asian Survey* 45(3): 414–436.

Roy, Denny. 2016. "The United States and the South China Sea: Front Line of Hegemonic Tension?" In *The South China Sea Dispute: Navigating Diplomatic and Strategic Tensions*, edited by Ian Storey and Lin Cheng-yi, 228–246. Singapore: ISEAS Publishing.

Schofield, Clive and Ian James Storey. 2009. *The South China Sea Dispute: Increasing Stakes and Rising Tensions*. Washington, DC: The Jamestown Foundation.

Scott, David. 2012. "Conflict Irresolution in the South China Sea." *Asian Survey* 52(6): 1019–1042.

Seah, Daniel. 2009. "The ASEAN Charter." *The International and Comparative Law Quarterly* 58(1): 197–212.

Severino, Rodolfo C. 2010. "ASEAN and the South China Sea." *Security Challenges* 6(2): 37–47.

Severino, Rodolfo C. 2007. "ASEAN Beyond Forty: Towards Political and Economic Integration." *Contemporary Southeast Asia* 29(3): 406–423.

Shirk, Susan. 2014. "The Domestic Context of Chinese Foreign Security Policies." In *Oxford Handbook of the International Relations of Asia*, edited by S. Pekkanen, J. Ravenhill and R. Foot, 391–410. Oxford: Oxford University Press.

Shoji, Tomotaka. 2014. "The South China Sea: A View from Japan." *NIDS Journal of Defense and Security* 127–141.

Simmons, Beth A. 2002. "Capacity, Commitment, and Compliance: International Institutions and Territorial Disputes." *Journal of Conflict Resolution* 46(6): 829–856.

Simon, Sheldon W. 2012. "Conflict and Diplomacy in the South China Sea." *Asian Survey* 52(6): 995–1018.

Singh, Abhijit. 2017. "Arbitration on the South China Sea – Implications for Maritime-Asia." In *Line in the Waters: The South China Sea Dispute and Its Implications for Asia*, edited by Abhijit Singh, 2–12. New Delhi: Observer Research Foundation.

Singh, Udai Bhanu. 2016. "South China Sea Arbitration Award: Implications for Southeast Asia." *Political Discourse* 2(2): 17–26.

Slaughter, Anne-Marie. 1995. "International Law in a World of Liberal States." *European Journal of International Law* 6(3): 503–538.

Smith, James McCall. 2000. "The Politics of Dispute Settlement Design: Explaining Legalism in Regional Trade Pacts." *International Organization* 54(1): 137–180.

Storey, Ian James. 1999. "Creeping Assertiveness: China, the Philippines and the South China Sea Dispute." *Contemporary Southeast Asia* 21(1): 95–118.

Subedi, Surya P. 2003. "Resolution of International Water Disputes: Challenges for the 21st Century." In *The Permanent Court of Arbitration/Peace Palace Papers: Resolution of International Water Disputes*, edited by The International Bureau of the Permanent Court of Arbitration, 6, 33–47. The Hague: Kluwer Law International.

Thayer, Carlyle A. 2013. "ASEAN, China and the Code of Conduct in the South China Sea." *SAIS Review of International Affairs* 33(2): 75–84.

Thayer, Carlyle A. 2011a. "Chinese Assertiveness in the South China Sea and Southeast Asian Responses." *Journal of Current Southeast Asian Affairs* 30(2): 77–104.

Thayer, Carlyle A. 2011b. "The Tyranny of Geography: Vietnamese Strategies to Constrain China in the South China Sea." *Contemporary Southeast Asia* 33(3): 348–369.

Thayer, Carlyle A. 2011c. "The United States, China and Southeast Asia." *Southeast Asian Affairs* 16–25.

Thayer, Carlyle A. 2010. "The United States and Chinese Assertiveness in the South China Sea." *Security Challenges* 6(2): 69–84.

Tibbetts, John. 2001. "Marine Science Sea Change in South China Sea." *Environmental Health Perspectives* 109(10): A470.

To, Lee Lai. 2003. "China, the USA and the South China Sea Conflicts." *Security Dialogue* 34(1): 25–39.

Tønnesson, Stein. 2006. "The South China Sea in the Age of European Decline." *Modern Asian Studies* 40(1): 1–57.

Tønnesson, Stein. 2002. "Why are the Disputes in the South China Sea So Intractable? A Historical Approach." *Asian Journal of Social Science* 30(3): 570–601.

Tønnesson, Stein. 2000. "Vietnam's Objective in the South China Sea: National or Regional Security?" *Contemporary Southeast Asia* 22(1): 199–220.

Tønnesson, Stein. 1991. *The Vietnamese Revolution of 1945: Roosevelt, Ho Chi Minh and de Gaulle in a World at War*. London: Sage Publications.

Tseng, Katherine Hui-Yi. 2017. *Rethinking South China Sea Disputes: The Untold Dimensions and Great Expectations*. London and New York: Routledge.

Tuan, Hoang Anh. 2017. "A Vietnamese Perspective on the South China Sea Dispute." In *The South China Sea Dispute: Navigating Diplomatic and Strategic Tensions*, edited by Ian Storey and Cheng-yi Lin, 186–204. New Delhi: Pentagon Press.

Turcsányi, Richard Q. 2018. *Chinese Assertiveness in the South China Sea: Power Sources, Domestic Politics, and Reactive Foreign Policy*. Basel, Switzerland: Springer International Publishing.

Valencia, Mark J. 1994. "Troubled Waters: Disputes in the South China Sea." *Harvard International Review* 16(2): 12–15.

Walker, Thomas C. and David L. Rousseau. 2016. "Liberalism: A Theoretical and Empirical Assessment." In *Routledge Handbook of Security Studies*, edited by Myriam Dunn Cavelty and Thierry Balzacq, 22–31. London and New York: Routledge.

Walt, Stephen M. 1998. "International Relations: One World, Many Theories." *Foreign Policy* 110: 29–46.

Waltz, Kenneth N. 2000. "Structural Realism After the Cold War." *International Security* 25(1): 5–41.

Waltz, Kenneth N. 1979 (reissued 2010). *Theory of International Politics*. Long Grove, IL: Waveland Press, Inc.

Wendt, Alexander. 1995. "Constructing International Politics." *International Security* 20(1): 71–81.

Wendt, Alexander. 1992. "Anarchy Is What States Make of It: The Social Construction of Power Politics." *International Organization* 46(2): 391–425.

Wenjuan, Nie. 2018. "China's Domestic Strategic Debate and Confusion Over the South China Sea Issue." *The Pacific Review* 31(2): 188–204.

Wu, Shicun and Keyuan Zou. 2016. *Arbitration Concerning the South China Sea: Philippines Versus China*. London: Routledge.

Yoshimatsu, Hidetaka. 2017. "China, Japan and the South China Sea Dispute: Pursuing Strategic Goals Through Economic and Institutional Means." *Journal of Asian Security and International Affairs* 4(3): 294–315.

Zangl, Bernhard, Achim Helmedach, Aletta Mondré, Alexander Kocks, Gerald Neubauer and Kerstin Blome. 2011. "Between Law and Politics: Explaining International Dispute Settlement Behavior." *European Journal of International Relations* 18(2): 369–401.

Zha, Daojiong. 2001. "Security in the South China Sea." *Alternatives: Global, Local, Political* 26(1): 33–51.

Zhang, Feng. 2017. "Assessing China's Response to the South China Sea Arbitration Ruling." *Australian Journal of International Affairs* 71(4): 440–459.

Zhao, Suisheng. 2015. "Rethinking the Chinese World Order: The Imperial Cycle and the Rise of China." *Journal of Contemporary China* 24(96): 961–982.

Zhou, Fangyin. 2016. "Between Assertiveness and Self-Restraint: Understanding China's South China Sea Policy." *International Affairs* 92(4): 869–890.

Newspapers/magazines/websites

Asia Maritime Transparency Initiative. 2019. "Malaysia Island Tracker." Accessed January 2, 2019. https://amti.csis.org/island-tracker/malaysia/

Asia Maritime Transparency Initiative. 2018a. "China Island Tracker." Accessed August 19, 2018. https://amti.csis.org/island-tracker/china/

Asia Maritime Transparency Initiative. 2018b. "Philippines Island Tracker." Accessed August 23, 2018. https://amti.csis.org/island-tracker/philippines/

Asia Maritime Transparency Initiative. 2018c. "Vietnam Island Tracker." Accessed December 26, 2018. https://amti.csis.org/island-tracker/vietnam/

Association of Southeast Asian Nations (ASEAN). 2014. "ASEAN Foreign Ministers' Statement on the Current Developments in the South China Sea." May 10. Accessed July 19, 2018. https://asean.org/wp-content/uploads/2012/05/24th-AFMs-Statement-on-SCS.pdf

Bader, Jeffrey A., Kenneth G. Lieberthal and Michael McDevitt. 2014. "Keeping the South China Sea in Perspective." *Brookings*, September 2. Accessed July 12, 2018. www.brookings.edu/research/keeping-the-south-china-sea-in-perspective/

Banlaoi, Rommel C. 2016. "Duterte Presidency: Shift in Philippine-China Relations?" *RSIS Commentaries*, May 20. Accessed January 2, 2019. www.rsis.edu.sg/rsis-publication/rsis/co16121-duterte-presidency-shift-in-philippine-china-relations/#.XPzbki17GYU

BenarNews. 2019. "US Suspicious of Beijing's Motive in South China Sea 'Code of Conduct'." *Radio Free Asia*, April 26. Accessed June 1, 2019. www.rfa.org/english/news/china/malaysia-southchinasea-04262019163855.html

Blanchard, Ben and Anthony Deutsch. 2016. "China Slams South China Sea Case as Court Set to Rule." *Reuters*, June 29. Accessed June 7, 2019. www.reuters.com/article/us-china-philippines-court-idUSKCN0ZF1QV?feedType=RSS&feedName=worldNews

Blanchard, Ben and Martin Petty. 2016. "China Vows to Protect South China Sea Sovereignty, Manila Upbeat." *Reuters*, July 14. Accessed July 28, 2018. www.reuters.com/article/us-southchinasea-ruling-stakes-idUSKCN0ZS02U

Brennan, Elliot. 2017. "Australia's 60-Year-Old South China Sea Prophecy Comes True." *The Diplomat*, June 12. Accessed June 2, 2019. https://thediplomat.com/2017/06/australias-60-year-old-south-china-sea-prophecy-comes-true/

British Broadcasting Corporation (BBC). 2016. "South China Sea: ASEAN Avoids Mention of China Ruling." July 25. Accessed July 29, 2018. www.bbc.com/news/world-asia-36878995

British Broadcasting Corporation (BBC). 2015. "Q&A: South China Sea Dispute." October 27. Accessed July 13, 2018. www.bbc.com/news/world-asia-pacific-13748349

Chan, Tara Francis. 2018. "China Is Not Even Pretending Anymore in the South China Sea – It Put 400 Buildings on One of the Disputed Islands." *Business Insider*, May 24. Accessed August 19, 2018. www.businessinsider.in/china-is-not-even-pretending-anymore-in-the-south-china-sea-it-put-400-buildings-on-one-of-the-disputed-islands/articleshow/64299765.cms

Chareonwongsak, Kriengsak. 2014. "ASEAN's Limits in Conflict Resolution in the Region." *Nanyang Technological University*. Accessed July 12, 2018. http://news.ntu.edu.sg/SAFNTU/Documents/Panel%201%20-%20Prof%20Kriengsak%20Chareonwongsak.pdf

Chaudhury, Dipanjan Roy. 2018. "South China Sea Verdict: All Parties Must Abide by International Order of Seas & Oceans, Says India." *Economic Times*, July 12. Accessed April 12, 2019. https://m.economictimes.com/news/defence/south-china-sea-verdict-all-parties-must-abide-by-international-order-of-seas-oceans-says-india/articleshow/53177912.cms

Cochrane, Joe. 2016. "Indonesia Confirms Seizing Fishing Boat in South China Sea, Defying Beijing." *New York Times*, June 20. Accessed June 21, 2018. www.nytimes.com/2016/06/21/world/asia/indonesia-south-china-sea-fishing.html?_r=0

Glaser, Bonnie S. 2015a. "Armed Clash in the South China Sea." *Council on Foreign Relations* Contingency Planning Memorandum No. 14." April 11. Accessed July 13, 2018. https://www.cfr.org/report/armed-clash-south-china-sea

Glaser, Bonnie S. 2015b. "Conflict in the South China Sea." *Council on Foreign Relations*, April 7. Accessed July 12, 2018. www.cfr.org/report/conflict-south-china-sea

Grossman, Derek. 2018. "The Quad Is Not Enough." *Foreign Policy*, October 19. Accessed June 13, 2019. https://foreignpolicy.com/2018/10/19/to-balance-china-call-vietnam-malaysia-philippines/

Haiquan, Zhu. 2016. "The South China Sea Dispute: Beijing's View." *New York Times*, May 31. Accessed June 17, 2018. www.nytimes.com/2016/06/01/opinion/the-south-china-sea-dispute-beijings-view.html?_r=0

Hart, Michael. 2018. "Brunei Abandons South China Sea Claim for Chinese Finance." *Geopolitical Monitor*, April 4. Accessed January 25, 2019. www.geopoliticalmonitor.com/brunei-abandons-south-china-sea-claim-for-chinese-finance/

Holland, Steve, John Chalmers and Raju Gopalakrishnan. 2017. "Trump Offers to Mediate in South China Sea Dispute." *Reuters*, November 12. Accessed March 10, 2019. www.reuters.com/article/us-trump-asia-southchinasea/trump-offers-to-mediate-in-south-china-sea-dispute-idUSKBN1DC01F?il=0

IANS. 2019. "Quad's 1st Ministerial Meeting Significant Elevation of Level." *The Economic Times*, September 27. Accessed September 29, 2019. https://economictimes.indiatimes.com/news/defence/quads-1st-ministerial-meeting-significant-elevation-of-level/articleshow/71324576.cms?from=mdr

Jennings, Ralph. 2019. "China, Wary of US, Pushes to Accelerate Accident Prevention Deal in Disputed Sea." *Voice of America (VOA)*, May 8. Accessed June 7, 2019. www.voanews.com/east-asia/china-wary-us-pushes-accelerate-accident-prevention-deal-disputed-sea

Johnson, Jesse. 2019. "Japan's Largest Warship Joins U.S. Carrier for Military Exercises in Disputed South China Sea." *The Japan Times*, June 12. Accessed June 13, 2019. www.japantimes.co.jp/news/2019/06/12/national/japans-largest-warship-joins-u-s-carrier-military-exercises-disputed-south-china-sea/#.XQIzxC17GYU

Khemara, Sok. 2018. "America Says South China Sea Code of Conduct Should 'Include International Principles'." *VOA Khmer*, August 9. Accessed April 6, 2019. www.voacambodia.com/a/america-says-south-china-sea-code-of-conduct-should-include-international-principles/4519204.html

Koring, Paul. 2015. "Tension Rising in South China Sea." *The Globe and Mail*, May 15. Accessed July 17, 2018. www.theglobeandmail.com/news/world/tension-rising-in-south-china-sea/article24440836/

Kraichitti, Krit. 2015. "Dispute Settlement Mechanisms for ASEAN Community: Experiences, Challenges and Way Forward." *Workshop on Trade and Investment ASEAN Law Association 12th General Assembly*, February 25–28. Accessed July 11, 2018. www.aseanlawassociation.org/12GAdocs/workshop5-thailand.pdf

Latiff, Rozanna. 2016. "Southeast Asian Countries Retract Statement Expressing Concerns on South China Sea." *Reuters*, June 15. Accessed June 19, 2016. www.reuters.com/article/us-southchinasea-asean-idUSKCN0Z10KX

Lendon, Brad and Katie Hunt. 2016. "China, Russia Begin Joint Exercises in South China Sea." September 13. Accessed November 20, 2018. http://edition.cnn.com/2016/09/12/asia/china-russia-south-china-sea-exercises/

Lo, Kinling. 2016. "China, Malaysia Seek to Resolve South China Sea Disputes with New Dialogue Mechanism." *South China Morning Post*, September 13. Accessed September 29, 2019. www.scmp.com/news/china/diplomacy/article/3026957/china-malaysia-seek-resolve-south-china-sea-disputes-new

Martin, Lisa. 2019. "Australian Navy Pilots Hit with Lasers During South China Sea Military Exercise." *The Guardian*, May 29. Accessed June 2, 2019. www.theguardian.com/australia-news/2019/may/29/australian-navy-pilots-hit-with-lasers-during-south-china-sea-military-exercise

Oceans & Law of the Sea, United Nations. 2013. "Declarations and Statements." Accessed June 9, 2019. www.un.org/depts/los/convention_agreements/convention_declarations.htm

Otto, Ben. 2016. "Indonesia's Widodo Wades into South China Sea Dispute." *Wall Street Journal*, June 23. Accessed June 24, 2018. www.wsj.com/articles/indonesias-widodo-wades-into-south-china-sea-dispute-1466683527

Packham, Colin. 2018. "Australia to Stress International Law in South China Sea Dispute." *Reuters*, March 13. Accessed February 25, 2019. www.reuters.com/article/us-asean-australia/australia-to-stress-international-law-in-south-china-sea-dispute-idUSKCN1GP0NM

Palatino, Mong. 2016. "How the Philippines Reacted to the South China Sea Ruling." *The Diplomat*, July 13. Accessed May 2, 2019. https://thediplomat.com/2016/07/how-the-philippines-reacted-to-the-south-china-sea-ruling/

Pant, Harsh V. and Kartik Bommakanti. 2018. "Can the Quad Deal with China?" *Deccan Herald*, November 26. Accessed June 13, 2019. www.deccanherald.com/specials/sunday-spotlight/can-quad-deal-china-704820.html

PCA Press Release. 2016. "The South China Sea Arbitration (The Republic of the Philippines v. The People's Republic of China)." *Permanent Court of Arbitration*, July 12. Accessed June 8, 2019. https://pca-cpa.org/en/news/pca-press-release-the-south-china-sea-arbitration-the-republic-of-the-philippines-v-the-peoples-republic-of-china/

Phillips, Tom. 2018. "Photos Show Beijing's Militarisation of South China Sea in New Detail." *The Guardian*, February 6. Accessed August 19, 2018. www.theguardian.com/world/2018/feb/06/photos-beijings-militarisation-south-china-sea-philippines

Phillips, Tom, Oliver Holmes and Owen Bowcott. 2016. "Beijing Rejects Tribunal's Ruling in South China Sea Case." *The Guardian*, July 12. Accessed June 9, 2019. www.theguardian.com/world/2016/jul/12/philippines-wins-south-china-sea-case-against-china

Pinghui, Zhuang. 2016. "G7 Leaders Vow to Send 'Clear Signal' Over South China Sea Row After Beijing Warns It Against 'Double Standards'." *South China Morning Post*, May 27. Accessed June 18, 2018. www.scmp.com/news/china/policies-politics/article/1955108/g7-leaders-vow-send-clear-signal-over-south-china-sea

Poling, Gregory B. 2013. "The South China Sea in Focus: Clarifying the Limits of Maritime Dispute." *Center for Strategic & International Studies*, July 17. Accessed July 12, 2018. www.csis.org/analysis/south-china-sea-focus

Press Trust of India (PTI). 2018a. "Australia Opposes 'Militarisation' in South China Sea, Says India's Role 'Critical'." *The Economic Times*, July 12. Accessed May 27, 2019. https://economictimes.indiatimes.com/news/defence/australia-opposes-militarisation-in-south-china-sea-says-indias-role-critical/articleshow/48773110.cms?from=mdr

Press Trust of India (PTI). 2018b. "China Holds Biggest Ever Military Drill in South China Sea." *The Times of India*, April 12. Accessed August 19, 2018. https://timesofindia.indiatimes.com/world/china/china-holds-biggest-ever-military-drill-in-south-china-sea/articleshow/63735943.cms

Press Trust of India (PTI). 2018c. "Opposed to Formation of Any Military Alliance in Indo-Pacific: Vietnam." *The Economic Times*, November 15. Accessed June 10, 2019. https://economictimes.indiatimes.com/news/defence/opposed-to-formation-of-any-military-alliance-in-indo-pacific-vietnam/articleshow/66636403.cms?from=mdr

Rajagopalan, Megha. 2016. "China Says More than 40 Countries Support Its Stance on South China Sea Dispute." *Reuters*, May 20. Accessed June 17, 2018. www.reuters.com/article/us-southchinasea-china-idUSKCN0YB1EO

Reuters Staff. 2018a. "China Unveils Monument to South China Sea Island Building." *Reuters*, April 24. Accessed August 19, 2018. www.reuters.com/article/us-china-southchinasea/china-unveils-monument-to-south-china-sea-island-building-idUSKBN1HV0Y8

Reuters Staff. 2018b. "China Urges Taiwan's Few Allies to Follow 'Irresistible Trend' of Recognizing Beijing." *Reuters*, March 8. Accessed August 17, 2018. www.reuters.com/article/us-china-parliament-taiwan/china-urges-taiwans-few-allies-to-follow-irresistible-trend-of-recognizing-beijing-idUSKCN1GK0KR

Santos, Matikas. 2016. "Philippines Wins Arbitration Case vs. China Over South China Sea." *INQUIRER.net*, July 12. Accessed July 27, 2018. http://globalnation.inquirer.net/140358/philippines-arbitration-decision-maritime-dispute-south-china-sea-arbitral-tribunal-unclos-itlos

Singh, Abhijit. 2016a. "India and the South China Sea Dispute." *The Diplomat*, March 1. Accessed June 10, 2019. https://thediplomat.com/2016/03/india-and-the-south-china-sea-dispute/

Singh, Abhijit. 2016b. "Why India's South China Sea Stand Matters." *Institute for Defense Studies and Analyses*, August 19. Accessed June 11, 2019. https://idsa.in/idsacomments/why-india-south-china-sea-stand-matters_asingh_190816

Singh, Sapna. 2019. "Naval Alliance Needs More Teeth." *The Pioneer*, March 30. Accessed June 13, 2019. www.dailypioneer.com/2019/columnists/naval-alliance-needs-more-teeth.html

Siregar, Kiki. 2020. "Chinese vessels leaving Natuna after days of stand-off with Indonesia." *Channel NewsAsia*, January 9. Accessed February 1, 2020. https://www.channelnewsasia.com/news/asia/natuna-china-indonesia-standoff-vessels-leave-12247302

The Philippine Star. 2016. "World Leaders React to South China Sea Ruling." July 13. Accessed July 28, 2018. www.philstar.com/headlines/2016/07/13/1602416/world-leaders-react-south-china-sea-ruling

The Times of India. 2018. "China Trying to Take Advantage of Ambiguous Situation and Enforce a Beijing Consensus in South China Sea." *The Times of India*, July 11. Accessed June 13, 2019. https://timesofindia.indiatimes.com/blogs/the-interviews-blog/china-trying-to-take-advantage-of-ambiguous-situation-and-enforce-a-beijing-consensus-in-south-china-sea/

United Nations Convention on the Law of the Sea. "Annex VII: Arbitration." Accessed June 9, 2019. www.un.org/depts/los/convention_agreements/texts/unclos/annex7.htm

Withers, Paul. 2019. "South China Sea: Beijing FURIOUS at Australia Claim Pilots Were Targeted by Lasers." *Daily Express*, May 30. Accessed June 4, 2019. www.express.co.uk/news/world/1134176/south-china-sea-military-drills-australia-pilots-lasers-us-china-war

Wong, Sue-Lin and Terrence Edwards. 2016. "China Tells Japan to Stop Interfering in South China Sea." *Reuters*, July 15. Accessed June 13, 2019. www.reuters.com/article/us-southchinasea-ruling-idUSKCN0ZV06F

Woon, Walter. 2012. "Dispute Settlement the ASEAN Way." *National University of Singapore*, December 11. Accessed July 10, 2018. https://cil.nus.edu.sg/wp-content/uploads/2010/01/WalterWoon-Dispute-Settlement-the-ASEAN-Way-2012.pdf

Yong, Charissa. 2018. "ASEAN, China Agree on Text to Negotiate Code of Conduct in South China Sea." *The Straits Times*, August 2. Accessed August 19, 2018. www.straitstimes.com/politics/asean-china-agree-on-text-to-negotiate-code-of-conduct-in-south-china-sea

Index

Note: Page numbers in *italics* refer to figures and those in **bold** refer to tables.

Act East Policy (AEP) 95
activities, toward SCS dispute solution *see* conflict management
Agreement Area in the South China Sea 30
Agreement on Fundamental Principles to Guide the Settlement of Sea Disputes 30
Agusman, Damos Dumoli 32, 49, 67–68, 83
Allied powers 23
Amador, Julio 32, 49, 67–68, 83
Andrews, Kevin 97
Aquino, Benigno, III 61, 74, 80, 83, 102
arbitral tribunal ruling 72–88; award 76–78; China's reaction 78–80; events before 74–76; judges 76; Philippines' response 80–81; UNCLOS and 72–74
Arif, Muhamad 49, 85, 103
ASEAN 3, 32; COC 15, 44–45, 46, 53, 57–58, 65, 69, 71, 82, 85, 92–93, 106–110; DOC 15, 43–45, 46, 47, 53, 57–58, 62, 69, 79, 82; joint initiatives by China and 38, 39, 43–45; track-1 diplomacy 28, 29
ASEAN Declaration of the South China Sea 90
ASEAN Defense Ministers Meeting Plus (ADMM Plus) 44
ASEAN Regional Forum (ARF) 12
ASEAN Way 10–12
Asia Maritime Transparency Initiative 34
assertiveness of China 39–40, **41**
Australia 96–97

Bai Meichu 20–21
Balakrishnan, Vivian 46
Bangladesh-India-Sri Lanka-Thailand Economic Cooperation (BISTEC) 94
Banlaoi, Rommel 50, 81, 102
Ban Than Reef/Zhongzhou Reef 55
Bata, Sidney Christopher T 84
Batongbacal, Jay 32, 49, 61, 83, 102
Baviera, Aileen 50, 60, 67, 82, 102, *112*
Bay of Bengal Initiative for Multi-Sectoral Technical and Economic Cooperation (BIMSTEC) 94, 95
Beckman, Robert 86, 103, *111*
Belt and Road Initiative (BRI) 51–53, 86
Bien Dong 31
bilateral activities, in SCS disputes 30
BIMSTEC 95
Bishop, Julie 97
British conquest 19
Brunei 1, 26, 31, 36, 87–88; bilateral ties with China 65–66, 71; claim and activities 65–66, 68; Exclusive Economic Zone (EEZ) 66, 68

CAC-301 (US State Department document) 25
CAC-308 (US State Department document) 25
Cairo Declaration 42
Cambodia, Laos, Myanmar, and Vietnam (CLMV) 94
Campbell, Piper 92
Cam Ranh Bay 25, 62
Carpio, Antonio T. 81, 101, 108, *110*
Chalermpalanupap, Termsak 86–87
Chaturvedy, Rajeev Ranjan 32, 103
Chen Duo 20
Chen Xiangmiao 45
Chiang Kai-shek 42

China: arbitral tribunal ruling and 72–88; ASEAN and 38, 39, 43–45; assertiveness 39–40, **41**; Australia and 96–97; Belt and Road Initiative (BRI) 51–53; conferences 29; delaying strategy 37–39; drilling rig 27; historical claims 34–37; India and 95, 96; island-building works 27; Middle Kingdom 34; military exercise 45–46; national interest 32; Nine-Dash Line 36, 39, 40, 41–43, 48–49, 58, 60, 64, 66–68, 75, 77, 78, 87–88, 90; outposts in Spratlys and Paracels 34; recent activities 45–47; as a regional power 32; Sansha city 27; UNDOALS on 74–75; US and 52–53
China Daily 93
China National Offshore Oil Corporation (CNOOC) 27, 30
Chinese Civil War 24
Chinese National Humiliation Map 20
Chua, Daniel 108
Clinton, Hillary 91
Code of Conduct (COC) 15, 44–45, 46, 53, 57–58, 65, 69, 71, 82, 85, 92–93, 106–110
Cold War 24–26, 90, 98, 103
colonial occupation of South China Sea (SCS) 17–21, **21–22**
Communist Party of China (CCP) 42, 53
conflict management 27–30; ASEAN Way of 12; bilateral 30; international 28; regional 28–30, *29*
constructivism/constructivists 8–10
Convention on the Limits of the Continental Shelf (CLCS) 28
Cot, Jean-Pierre 76

Dagat Kanlurang Pilipinas 31
Dai Bingguo 91
Daily Inquirer 45
Declaration of Paris of 1856 18
Declaration on the Conduct of Parties in the South China Sea (DOC) 15, 43–45, 46, 47, 53, 57–58, 62, 69, 79, 82
decolonization 23–26
De Lima, Leila 81
Diplomatic Academy of Vietnam 29
Djalal, Hasjim 29, 33, 48, 84, 102
DOC *see* Declaration on the Conduct of Parties in the South China Sea (DOC)
Duterte, Rodrigo 60–61, 67–68, 81–88, 101, 102
Duterte Presidency: Shift in Philippine-China Relations (Banlaoi) 81
Duterte's Geopolitical Game-Play (Heydarian) 82

East Asia Summit (EAS) 62
East Timor dispute 12
economic corridors 51
Eleven-Dash Line 42
Encomienda, Alberto 32, 44, 67
European Union (EU) 3, 33
Exclusive Economic Zone (EEZ) 13, 30, 36, 77–78
Expanded ASEAN Maritime Forum (EAMF) 95

Fiery Cross Reef 46
fisheries 33
Five Power Treaty 21
foreign policy of Duterte administration 82
France 19
Freedomland 59
Freedom of Navigation Operations (FONOP) 90–91

Gao Huchen 52
Garcia, Carlos 35–36
geopolitical issues 32
Global Times 45
Greater Mekong Subregion 39
Guan, Kwa Chong 50, 103
Gulf of Tonkin 30
Guotu, Zhuang 45

Hai Yang Shi You-981 37
Han dynasty 36
Heydarian, Richard Javad 82
Hiep, Le Hong 32, 48, 62–63, 68, 86, 103, *113*
Hikmahanto, Juwana 49, 84
Hong Kong 26
Hong Lei 76–77
Hongzhou, Zhang 48, 87

India 93–96; Act East Policy (AEP) 95; ASEAN and 94, 95, 96; BISTEC and

94; CLMV and 94; Look East Policy (LEP) 95; US and 95
Indochina 19
Indonesia 3, 12, 17, 19, 23, 68, 71, 86, 88; Malaysia and 23, 28; Nine-Dash Line and 67; position of 66–67; US and 103; Vietnam's maritime claims 61; workshops on the SCS 28–29, 38, 56, 98
Institute of Ocean and Earth Sciences in Kuala Lumpur 29
International Conference on Cooperation in Dealing with Non-traditional Security Issues in the South China Sea 29
International Convention for the Protection of Submarine Cables 18
International Court of Arbitration 20
International Court of Justice (ICJ) 12, 13, 14, 28
international law 13–14
international level activities, toward SCS dispute solution 28
International Maritime Organization 18
international relations theories 3–10; constructivism 4, 8–10; liberalism 4, 6–8; realism 4–6
International Tribunal for the Law of the Sea (ITLOS) 12, 13, 28, 73, 83
International Workshop on the Marine Environmental Change of the South China Sea 29
International Workshop on the South China Sea 29
islands: artificial 72, 73; *vs.* rocks 48–49, 72–73, 78
Itu Aba Island 25

James Shoal 20, 21, 35
Japan 97–99; advancement in the SCS 21; invasion of China 21; invasion of Manchuria 19; oil imports 26; World War II 23–24, 97–98
Japanese invasion of China 21
Joint Intelligence Committee of Australia 96
Joint Working Group (JWG) 36, 39, 41–43

Kalaya 26
Kembara, Gilang 65–66, 85
Kerry, John 92
Kraft, Herman Joseph 101
Kuomintang (KMT) 55

Law of the Sea, The (Churchill and Lowe) 13
Law of the Sea Convention (LOSC) 13–14; Annex VIII of 14; Annex VII of 14; Annex VI of 13; Article 279 of 13; Article 280 of 13; Article 284 of 13
"Law on the Territorial Waters and Their Contiguous Areas" 42
Lean, Collin Koh Swee 50, 66, 87, 103, 108
Le Hai Binh 78
Liaoning 45
liberalism 6–8
Li Jie 46
Li Keqiang 98
Liu Zhenmin 79
Look East Policy (LEP) 95
Louisa Reef 26

Malaysia 1, 31, 36, 61, 87; as anti-communist federation 23; ASEAN and 69, 70; China's economic relations 67, 68, 85, 86; claim and activities 63–65; formation of 23; Indonesia and 28; Philippines and 84; Spratly Islands and 26; Vietnam and 63–65
Malik, Mohan 34
Manchuria, Japanese invasion of 19
Mao Zedong 24
Map of Chinese Islands in the South China Sea, The 20
Marcos, Ferdinand 26
maritime issues 32
Mekong-Ganga Cooperation 95
Mensah, Thomas A. 76
Middle Kingdom 34
Middle Rocks 28
military exercise of China 45–46
Minjindang (MJD) 57
Mischief Reef 30, 34, 58, 64, 67, 69, 74, 77, 79, 90
Muhibat, Shafiah Fifi 103
Musor, Gonaranao B. 108

Nan Hai 31
Nanning-Singapore economic corridor 39
National Institute for South China Sea Studies 45

Natuna Island 66, 68, 86, 88
Naval, Jaime B. 50, 82
New China Construction Atlas 20
New York Times 75
Nine-Dash Line 36, 39, 40, 41–43, 48–49, 58, 60, 64, 66–68, 75, 77, 78, 87–88, 90

Obama, Barack 52, 91
Oegroseno, Arif Havas 107, *112*
"One Belt, One Road" (OBOR) 51, 52
Opium War 19

Papa, Alcuin 83
Paracel Islands 19; dispute over 20, 31–32; French invasion of 20; World War II 23–25, 54, 97–98
Pattiradjawane, Rene L. 50
Pawlak, Stanislaw 76
Pedra Branca/ Pulau Batu Puteh islets 28
People's Liberation Army (PLA) 37, 40
People's Liberation Army Navy (PLA-N) 37, 38, 40, 91
Permanent Court of Arbitration (PCA) 2, 14
Petro Vietnam 30
Philippine National Oil Company (PNOC) 30
Philippines 1–3, 28, 30–33, 40, 44, 47, 55, 58, 108; arbitral tribunal award 2, 72–88; ASEAN and 23, 68–69; claim and activities 59–61; Duterte administration and 81–88; EU and the G-7 support 89; independence 23, 25; Japan's bilateral ties with 98; Mischief Reef incident 30, 58, 64, 69; Spanish-American War 19; Spanish occupation 19; Spratly Islands 25–26, 35–36; tripartite agreement 30; US and 25, 101–102; *see also* Scarborough Shoal
Pioneer 100
Potsdam Proclamation 42
pursue the case through arbitration (PCA) 82

Qing dynasty 19
Quadrilateral Security Dialogue (QSD) 99–101

realism 4–6
regional activities, toward SCS dispute solution 28–30, *29*
Regional Comprehensive Economic Partnership 108
Resolution of International Water Disputes: Challenges for the 21st Century (Subedi) 14
Review Committee for Land and Water Maps of China 20
Richardson, John 93

S. Rajaratnam School of International Studies at Nanyang Technological University 29
San Francisco Peace Conference 23, 25
Sansha city 27
Scarborough Shoal 1, 25–26, 27, 31, 32, 34, 60, 67, 68, 74, 75, 76, 77, 79, 82, 83, 102
Schriver, Randall 93
Security Council (SC) 28, 49
Shen Jinlong 93
Sim, Christine 108
Singapore 3, 19, 21, 23, 28, 29, 39, 46, 92, 103
Singh, V. K. 94
Sino-Japanese Peace Treaty 23
Sino-Japanese War 20
Song Zhongping 46
Soons, Alfred H. A. 76
South China Sea (SCS) 1–3; colonial occupation of 17–21, **21–22**; efforts toward dispute solution 27–30; fundamental problems 31–33; geography and location 1; lingering challenges 30–31; overlapping claims and maritime flashpoint *29*; prospect of disputes 105; recent developments 26–27; theoretical debates and 105–106; theorization 106–107
"South China Sea, The: Sustaining Ocean Productivities, Maritime Communities, and the Climate" 29
Southeast Asia 28
South Ledge 28
Soviet Union 24–25
Spain 19
Spanish-American War of 1898 19
Spratly Islands 25–27; British claim 19; dispute over 20, 31, 32; French claim 19–20; significance and issues 26–27; World War II 23–25, 42, 54, 59–60, 97–98
Sri Vijaya 17
Straits of Malacca 17
Subedi, Surya P. 14

Taiwan 1, 17, 85–87, 105; ASEAN claimant states and 32, 68, 85–86; claim and position 54–55; identity crisis 71; Japanese occupation 19, 21, 23; one-China policy 56–59, 71, 87; Pratas Islands and 31–32; sovereignty or sovereign state 67, 68; Spratly Islands and 20, 26, 61, 62; Taiping Island and 26, 67, 77
Taiwan Strait 1, 54
Tavares, Jose Antonio Morato 32
territorial disputes 31–32
Tibet 40, 91
Tønnesson, Stein 18
track-1 diplomacy 28, 29
track-2 diplomacy 28–29
trade 31
Tran, Teresa 33, 101, 107
Treaty of Amity and Cooperation (TAC) 10, 11, 12
Tripartite Agreement for Joint Marine Seismic Undertaking 30
Triton Island 27, 37
Trump, Donald 60, 92, 100, 101, 102, 103, 104
Trung Sa Island 26
Tseng, Katherine Hui-Yi 48, 85

United Nations (UN) 25; Convention on the Limits of the Continental Shelf (CLCS) 28; limitation of 28; Security Council (SC) 28, 49
United Nations Convention on the Law of the Non-navigational Uses of International Watercourses *see* Watercourses Convention
United Nations Convention on the Law of the Sea (UNCLOS) 2, 27, 28, 33, 36, 40, 42, 45, 58, 60, 64, 65, 66, 68, 69; Annex VII 47, 73, 76, 80, 84; Annex VIII 73; Article 282 73; Article 287 73; Article 298 79; Article 311(2) 74; China's ratification of 38; coastal states under 72; India and 94–95; islands *vs.* rocks 48–49, 72–73, 78; maritime claims under 47; sovereignty issues and 85; tribunal ruling 72–88; US and 89, 101, 102–103
United Nations Division for Ocean Affairs and the Law of the Sea (UNDOALS) 74–75
United States (US) 101–104; as an extra-regional power 32; Asian pivot agenda 91; China and 52–53; national interest 32; naval vessels 91; policy 90–93; role 101–104
USNS *Impeccable* 91
US-PHL Military Bases Agreement 102
US State Department 24–25

Vermonte, Philips J. 107
Vietnam 1–2, 40, 58; anti-China protests/riots 27, 57; ASEAN and 43, 47, 67, 68, 69; Cam Ranh Bay 25, 62; claim and activities 30, 43, 47–48, 61–63; communist party-to-party ties 86, 87; Japan and 98; Malaysia and 63–65; military clash with China 55, 56; Nine-Dash Line and 41, 42; oil projects 38, 40, 67; Paracel Islands 25, 31, 36–37, 86–87; PCA and 78; Philippines and 67–68; PRC and 56; Quad and 100; Spratly Islands 25, 26, 31–32; US and 58, 103–104
Vietnam Lawyers Association 29
Vietnam War 23, 24, 25, 50

Wang Yi 46–47, 52, 93
Watercourses Convention 14
Wisnu, Dinna 32
Wolfrum, Rüdiger 76
workshops and conferences 28–29
Workshops on Managing Potential Conflicts in the South China Sea 28–29
World War II 23–25, 42, 54, 59, 97–98

Xi Jinping 45, 51, 52, 79

Yasuhisa Kawamura 98

Zhang Yesui 52
Zheng He 17
Zhongzhou Reef *see* Ban Than Reef/ Zhongzhou Reef
Zhou Enlai 35
Zhu Haiquan 75–76
Zhu Rongji 61

www.ingramcontent.com/pod-product-compliance
Ingram Content Group UK Ltd.
Pitfield, Milton Keynes, MK11 3LW, UK
UKHW011019180926
475701UK00004B/833